Fine Art of
America's Fairways

FEATURING PAINTINGS OF AMERICA'S
FINEST ACCESSIBLE GOLF COURSES

Special Introduction *By Judy Bell*
Past President of The USGA

Foreword *By Reg Murphy*
Past President of The USGA

The Legacy of American Golf *By Sidney Matthew*

Compiled and Edited *By Michael E. Ventola, Jr.*

Published By

Fine Art of the Fairways, Inc.

Atlanta   Pinehurst

Acknowledgements

I would like to thank many people because without them this book could not have been possible. To my partners in Fine Art of the Fairways, a finer group of true gentlemen could not be found. To Governor Carl Sanders, your guidance and support was greatly appreciated. To Tom Camp, a man who was destined to become an integral part of this project. Thanks, Tom, for asking me what I did for a living. To Randy Hasty, for a very important introduction. To all of "my" artists, thank you for your incredible talent and support. To Tom, Illana, and Brian Stewart, thank you for making your home mine during this project. To Andie Rose, for all of the changes that you had to endure. To Suzanne, Alex, Mandy, and especially Michael Gray, you are always in my thoughts and will forever be my inspiration.

But four people above all will forever have my gratitude. To Barbara Ventola, your faith in your son never wavered and kept me going. To my sister, Barbara Brower, who came back into my life in the most trying of times and saved me. To my brother Bob, for supporting me through the dark times. And to my father, who introduced me to both fine art and the game of golf.

Thank you all.

Michael E. Ventola, Jr.

Michael E. Ventola, Jr.
President, Fine Art of the Fairways, Inc.

Contributing Writers - Tom Stewart, Barbara Brower, Wayne Aaron, Carl Trieshmann, Will Katz, Rick Franzman, and Michael E. Ventola, Jr.

Design and Layout - Andie Rose Design, Southern Pines, NC

Editing and Proofreading - Steve Hamelman, Conway, SC

Color Separations - Digital Color Image, - Pennsauken, NJ

Printing - RR Donnelley & Sons Co.

All inquiries should be addressed to:
Fine Art of the Fairways, Inc., 9550 Huntcliff Trace, Atlanta, GA 30350
888-249-7710

Library of Congress Cataloging-in-Publication Data on File

ISBN 0-9665137-0-3

The excitement of "Fine Art of America's Fairways" goes well beyond being a golf or art book. It affords us a wonderful look at some of the truly great golfing places in America, with one common denominator - each illustrated course is accessible to all. It's important to note that there are more courses open to everyone in this country than ever before, and this number far exceeds the number of private courses. To find this outstanding illustration of accessible golf is an extra bonus. You will discover great courses by any measure, well-represented in this book.

One such course, affectionately called "Bethpage Black," will host the U. S. Open Championship in the year 2002. Take my word for it, the "Black," will go down in the record book as producing a great champion over the best possible test. More than 120,000 rounds are played over the four courses at Bethpage each year, with standing room only. Another course is "Black Wolf Run" in Kohler, Wisconsin, which hosted the 1998 U.S. Women's Open. This course has breathtaking views and promises to test every player's imagination.

Each day, a new course is being built in our country and most of these are accessible to all golfers. So sit back and enjoy another memorable golf experience as you browse through the pages of "Fine Art of America's Fairways."

Judy Bell
Past President USGA

Judy Bell
By Kenneth Reed

INTRODUCTION

The fine art that is produced by an artist creating a masterpiece from a blank canvas ... a golf course architect sculpting a work of art from an undeveloped landscape. Passion, feeling, and vision describe both artist and architect alike, hence the inspiration behind the conception of "Fine Art of America's Fairways."

In the initial stage of development, our mission was to find artists who could capture the essence of a beautiful landscape where a golf hole "happened to get in the way." Then the decision had to be made about which courses to include from the hundreds that came to mind. The unfortunate perception of most golfers is that their dream courses, the ones that inspire awe, are unattainable to the vast majority because of private club status. And then, of course, there is every golfer's dream of taking a pilgrimage to Scotland or Ireland. For years, the isles have been recognized as a golf destination extraordinaire, and deservedly so, but they are still unattainable for many. But what about a pilgrimage right here on American soil? Contrary to common perceptions, there are many courses that we see on televised USGA, PGA, and LPGA Tour events, and other forms of media, that are accessible to all of us. Organizations such as the World Golf Foundation, First Tee, the USGA Fellowship Program, and the For The Good Of The Game Program, are promoting the accessibility and affordability of golf to the masses through instruction, youth programs, and availability of equipment. In keeping with the spirit and timing of these organizations, "Fine Art of America's Fairways" takes its readers on a journey, led by America's best golf artists, to some of this country's finest accessible golf courses, and in doing so, shatters the myth of golf's exclusivity.

All of the golf courses featured in this book, including five of the next six U.S. Open host sites, are open to the public. The vast diversity present in courses throughout the different regions of this country makes for an abundance of incredible golf experiences right here. From the stunning autumn foliage that abounds in Maine to the rock-hard lava fields of Hawaii, and from the majestic mountains and stark, dry deserts of Arizona and California to the wetlands of the Carolina and Georgia coasts, there is a veritable cornucopia of golf venues to be found in our country. Privy to such a variety of spectacular landscapes and colorful surroundings in your homeland, you may find yourself humming a few bars of "America the Beautiful."

The ensemble of outstanding golf artists that guide your tour through these magnificent places to play brings an intangible element to their work that a photograph just can not match – and this element is feeling. This book is not a travel guide or a "best of" book. Rather, it is a look at the work of some of the best golf course architects in the world – designers such as Robert Trent Jones, Tom Fazio, Jack Nicklaus, Donald Ross, A.W. Tillinghast, Alister MacKenzie, and Tom Weiskopf – as seen through the sensitive eyes of some of America's best painters. These artists leave an indelible impression on you with their brush strokes. You will be able to feel as though you could step onto each hole through the painting, arousing the longing to seek out the spot if you've never been there, or achieving instant recognition if you have.

Each course has a unique story to tell of how it was born, from the land on which it was created, to the dream of its owners, to its accomplishments and accolades. Some of the stories you read in these pages are set in golf lore history; others, though brand-new, may also be legendary someday. The courses presented are all special, made even more attractive by the fact that you can play every one of them.

We at Fine Art of the Fairways encourage you to take a good look around you the next time you play. You may just find that your score is not the only point worthy of attention. We hope that after reading this book you will find the splendor in the beauty that surrounds every swing of a golf club, embodying the American Golf Experience.

First Lesson
By Bucky Bowles

TABLE OF CONTENTS

Ray Ellis

FINE ART OF AMERICA'S FAIRWAYS
EAST

Ray Ellis

Paul Milosevich

FOREWORD
REG MURPHY

The early painters loved the faces and body languages of golfers. Agonized expressions and contorted postures were common. No surprise there; golf is the most private of sports agonies because there is nobody to share the blame. That the artists captured the emotions so poignantly enlightens us to the raging war of nerves inside.

The painters also utilized dramatic color. When you look at 19th-century art, you find that golfers wore red jackets. This was to warn Sunday strollers along the Scottish links that they should beware of the golfers in their midst, whacking leather-covered balls of stuffed feathers.

Why people and not landscapes? Perhaps it was because golf landscapes are like no other. The great British landscape artists like Frederick Turner used turbulent skies, dramatic water movement, towering cliffs for their focal points.

Golf, as everybody knows, is different. Golf cannot be played in an ugly place. It uses yellow sunlight, verdant grass, splotches of sand, and bordering trees in harmony to create its beauty.

Rain Gear
By Ray Ellis

Ladies' Day
By Walt Spitzmiller

To be sure, the golfer chooses at the critical moment one precise target in that scene and attempts to deliver his ball to that exact spot without wayward detours. Once he or she has struck the shot, however, the senses are inclined to wander again to the fragrance of new-mown grass or the babbling of a meandering brook. The non-golfing painter must have been puzzled by this lack of one specific focal point for the scene. (No, the breeze-blown tiny flag in the distance would not have seemed the focal point!)

Both photographers and painters eventually learned that the vistas must be presented in unusual ways. The great modern photographers like Brian Morgan and Tony Roberts use near-dawn and nearly-dusk shadows to give perspective and depth to their images. They struggle to help us understand the texture of the land where the game is played. The realism of their work always is a joy to behold.

But paintings! Those of us who dabble with paintbrushes fail to understand this: How do the talented artists manage to convey understanding and emotion with something so inanimate as a few bristles and a little pigment stirred with a small amount of liquid? Who among us understands why our minds go wandering to the clubs in the trunk of the car at the mere sight of a sketch of cross-hatched grass plopped in the midst of sandy depressions? What golfer fails to respond to the thought of four hours in the sun and wind and exhilaration of the game?

Before the paintings, there must be structure. God gets the first credit. Somebody asked a caddie at St. Andrews, "Who was the architect of this course?" To which the old fellow replied, "It was the Man up there that did it."

Yes, but some mere mortal must take what God has created and apply the touches that make it a course. Those who are inspired mystify the rest of us. I once saw Ben Crenshaw pick up a potato chip and say in all seriousness, "That would make a great shape for a green." The modern American architects included

Gin Game
By Ray Ellis

in any list of superlatives would name Tom Fazio, Rees Jones, Pete Dye, and Arthur Hills. They have added immeasurably to the visual quality of our courses. But to single them out is to create an injustice for the dozens of others who also have provided marvelous places for us to play. As the most obvious sites have been consumed, the challenge to build natural, beautiful, and serene courses has become even greater.

Some critics of the game (and the art) have claimed that it is a game only for the rich. Ah, the blindness of the critics. The United States Golf Association's research indicates that more than 80 percent of the 20 million-plus golfers play at daily fee courses, not exclusive country clubs. And many of those of us who now play at private clubs learned the game on courses open to all comers. In fact, the United States Open and other national championships are being moved to public golf courses as a new century approaches.

True origins of the game are lost in mists of time not unlike some April mornings when the flagstick is barely visible through the fog. The golfers would have been required to brave blustery weather and bone-chilling drizzles to get to the town, for that is the nature of the area along the North Sea. Came the much-anticipated calm, sunny day and they were joined on the links by the townsfolk out for a walk. Artists captured that—the people in the landscape—before they painted the courses with anything like the skill of today.

Artists are attracted naturally to both nature's beauty and man's struggles with it. As the game developed, it changed slowly. The early courses that we love (Scottish, mostly) were developed with virtually no help from engineers who moved dirt. Nor did they have the benefit of landscapers, arborists, or even expert greenkeepers. Theirs was the natural beauty of the land. That sometimes rugged land eventually beguiled the painters into practicing their art simply because it was an intriguing blend of human emotion and natural beauty.

Nobody can deny that carefully landscaped areas enhance the visual quality of golf courses. As the architects came to insert their lakes and bunkers and shrubs, the courses took on new color and clearer definition. In the words of noted sports artist LeRoy Neiman, "The artist just doesn't walk out on a golf course with a sketch pad to portray a particular golfer, or tournament, or course. Straightaway, he is confronted by an awesome greenscape equally as intimidating and challenging to him as it is to the golfer on his mission."

The artist's interpretation of what he or she sees opens our eyes to new vistas, tells us new things about our sport, engages us in the continuing discussion of what makes an appealing course. We are obliged to them for what they contribute to our enjoyment of golf.

— Reg Murphy

The Walker
By Paul Milosevich

GREENSIDE ARTIST
By Walt Spitzmiller

BIOGRAPHIES

Walt Spitzmiller

Walt Spitzmiller is one of the world's foremost sporting artists. He has dedicated much of his finest work to portraying the many aspects of the game of golf, from its rich traditions to its heroes and its most memorable competitions.

Walt is perhaps best recognized for his many contributions to "Golf Magazine" and "Sports Illustrated," for which he has completed over 125 paintings. He is currently Chief Contributing Artist at "Senior Golfer Magazine."

A 21-year resident of Redding, Connecticut, Walt is a graduate of Washington University School of Fine Arts in St. Louis. He works exclusively in oils and has received hundreds of national and international honors. His recent exhibits include a one-man show at The United States Golf Association. His work is also in the collections of the Baseball Hall of Fame, The Smithsonian Institute, The American Museum of Illustration, The Rodeo Hall of Fame Museum, the PGA Tour, and many corporate and private collections throughout the United States, Europe, and Asia.

CREDITS:

Painting: Francis Ouimet

    Ben Hogan

    Jack Nicklaus

    Arnold Palmer

    Mickey Wright

    Babe Zaharias

    Kathy Whitworth

    Patty Berg

    Nancy Lopez

    Greenside Artist

    Ladies Day

    Golf Widow

Ronal Parlin

I knew from the age of eight years that I wanted to be an artist. I was fortunate to grow up in a large and talented family. The material things we lacked were more than outweighed by the music, art, and invention that filled our days.

Because our home was small, we were often sent out-of-doors to play. This was the beginning of my fascination with the Maine landscape and I continually strive to capture its spirit in oil.

My father taught us to fish and many were the days you could find me heading down the hill to the nearest trout brook. My love of brooks and streams has carried over into my painting. The perfect work day for me is to be painting alongside a stony brook or river, with a few breaks during the day to catch a fish or two!

I am a dedicated plein-air painter. The greatest lessons come to me when I am in nature's presence and I am eager and ready to listen.

I live in rural Temple, Maine, with my artist wife Annette and our three children. The countryside here offers me an endless supply of magnificent subject matter. My work can be found in numerous private and corporate collections including Sears Roebuck, Dean Witter, and Maryland Bank of North America. I am currently showing work at Maine's Massachusetts House Galleries in Lincolnville, Maine.

CREDITS:

Painting: Sugarloaf

Linda Hartough

Since focusing her skills as a landscape painter to recreate some of the world's most beautiful golf holes, Linda Hartough has become recognized as one of golf's leading artists. So extraordinary and realistic is her attention to detail that her oil paintings seem to come alive with a clarity that surpasses the camera.

Her work has gained international fame. She is the only artist ever commissioned by the United States Golf Association and The Royal and Ancient Golf Club of St. Andrews to do the annual official paintings and prints for the U.S. Open and British Open Championships. She has painted prestigious golf courses from the United States to Scotland to Hong Kong. Her paintings are so admired that they have earned a place on two ABC Television Golf Specials on famous golf holes, hosted by Jack Nicklaus. Her paintings are in the collections of such famous clubs as Augusta National, Pine Valley, Pinehurst, and Laurel Valley. Hartough originals are also included in the private collections of Jack Nicklaus, Robert Trent Jones, and Rees Jones.

A confirmed artist since the age of six, Linda was raised in the picturesque countryside of Wilmington, Delaware, and Louisville, Kentucky. Much of her early career was spent in Chicago where, after receiving her Fine Arts degree from the prestigious School of the Art Institute of Chicago in 1970, she made a living by selling her paintings locally. In 1980, Linda moved to South Carolina near Hilton Head, where in addition to painting landscapes, portraits, and horses, she raised miniature horses.

In 1984, she was commissioned to paint the 13th hole at Augusta National, thus beginning her golf landscape career. After an overwhelming response to her work at the 1988 PGA Show in Orlando, Linda focused her career entirely on golf landscapes.

Linda's approach to capturing a great golf hole is by spending a week or more at each course, taking photographs at different times of the day to capture all possible lights. She then figures out what is important or memorable in each view of a hole and makes sure this is included in the painting. Her memory serves as a less objective image of the hole. The combination of the two provides the unique view found in each of her paintings.

"I really enjoy painting golf landscapes. There are some of the most beautiful and varied landscapes in the world combined with a deep, historical sense of tradition that transcends time. The painting is a success when both elements emerge."

Currently Linda lives with her husband Ed on over 200 acres of remote, beautiful Low Country land which is managed for quail, dove, wild turkey, and deer and is also home to a herd of miniature horses, two llamas, and four dogs.

For more information contact:

The Linda Hartough Gallery
PO Box 21325, Hilton Head Island, SC 29925
Tel: (843) 836-3821 FAX: (843) 836-3249
Toll Free Orderline: 888-333-1525
Website: www.hartough.com
E-Mail: hartough@hargray.com

CREDITS:

Paintings:	Pebble Beach, 7th Hole
	Pebble Beach, 17th Hole
	Harbour Town, 18th Hole
	Pinehurst, Number 2, 5th Hole
	Harbour Town, Remarque
Sketches:	Pebble Beach, 7th Hole
	Pinehurst Clubhouse
	Gene Sarazen

Ray Ellis

Ray Ellis is widely recognized for the originality of his paintings. His work has been sought out for many museum and private collections in the United States and abroad.

Ellis was born in Philadelphia and attended the famed Philadelphia Museum School of Art. His first one-man show was held in 1947 at the Pennsylvania Academy of Fine Arts.

After serving four years in the Coast Guard during WWII, he founded his own advertising agency in New Jersey and New York, but continued to paint in his spare time. During this period he was elected to the American Watercolor Society, and his works were widely exhibited and received numerous honors.

In 1969, Ellis was able to devote all his time to painting. In 1974, he moved south to Hilton Head Island, South Carolina, and then to Savannah, Georgia. Only recently has he resettled in the north, where he maintains a home and studio on Martha's Vineyard.

He has collaborated on many fine art books. Ellis and Walter Cronkite published three books on Amercia's coastlines: "South by Southeast," "North by Northeast," and "Westwind." In 1992, Ellis teamed up with golf journalist Ben Wright on "The Spirit of Golf." Paintings of Savannah and Martha's Vineyard have been published in separate volumes: "Ray Ellis' Savannah & the Low Country" and "Martha's Vineyard: An Affectionate Memoir." Forthcoming titles include "At the Water's Edge," "Painting America's Coasts," and "The Road to Ballybunion."

Ellis is represented in fine galleries across the United States and in London, England, where his shows of American and foreign subjects have been highly successful. He participates in several one-man shows and invitational exhibitions around the country each year.

"He has the ability to see the beauty of almost anything and capture it in his painting."
Walter Cronkite

"His work is alive with presence."
David Shirey, "The New York Times"

COMPASS PRINTS, INC./RAY ELLIS GALLERY
205 W. Congress Street, Savannah, GA 31401
(912) 234-3537 FAX (912) 234-5530
E-Mail: HYPERLINK mail to: EllisGal@ix.netcom.com
Internet Site: http://www.rayellis.com

CREDITS:

Paintings: Spring Foursome at Greenbrier
             The Old White Course, Greenbrier
             TPC Sawgrass
             Rain Gear
             15th at Harbourtown
             Gin Game
             Testing the Wind
             Practice Swing

Adriano Manocchia

Adriano Manocchia is an artist by vocation and a sporting artist by choice. His earlier career as a photojournalist had all the glamour and excitement one could imagine. Adriano photographed presidents, Formula One races, flew on blimps, and landed on aircraft carriers. He captured on camera rare interviews with such celebrities as Tennessee Williams and Muhammad Ali. But while he flew in experimental flying cars, drove tanks across the desert, or flew above the clouds recording mid-air refueling missions, creativity was already shaping a new career.

Adriano's interest in art was sparked during a visit to the Southwest. His brilliant artistic talent found its expression in superb paintings of animals, landscapes, sporting scenes, and golf images where nature and man coexist. The peacefulness of his oil paintings has become his trademark, along with the "transparency of his waterscapes," as Peter Friederici, a noted writer, stated in an article which appeared in "Wildlife Art": "Water is at the center of his art. It laps and ripples, flows slowly toward a rocky dropoff in a trout stream, or beats in furious waves against an ocean beach. It reflects the light of the sky and the colors of its surroundings, but still has its mass and bulk. Wherever it is, wherever it is going, the water in a Manoccia painting is very much alive."

His association with the golf world began with the request from the USGA to create two paintings: "The Honors Course", and "Eighth at Pebble Beach." These images immediately attracted the attention of art and golf connoisseurs. A masterful rendition of "TPC Sawgrass" was purchased by the PGA Tour for their headquarters, while Club Corp. of America commissioned a painting of Barton Creek. Ben Crenshaw endorsed one of Adriano's paintings, which was reproduced into a limited edition print along with four other successful images: "Pinehurst,"

"Harbourtown Golf Links," "TPC Sawgrass," and "TPC Scottsdale." He also created seven paintings for the book "Fine Art of Georgia's Fairways," which offered Adriano the freedom to express his view of each course, resulting in some of his most powerful paintings. For Easton Press, Adriano created pencil sketches and two paintings reproduced as the frontispiece for the reissue of Harvey Peneck's "Little Red Book Golf Classics."

Adriano's originals are represented by such fine galleries as J.N. Bartfield (NY), Trailside Americana (WY), The Sporting Gallery (VA), The McEwan Fine Art Gallery (Scotland), and The Sporting Life (C).

CREDITS:

Paintings:	Sea Island
	TPC Sawgrass
	Innisbrook
	Pinehurst
	White Columns
	Barton Creek
	TPC Scottsdale
	Bay Harbor
	Duke University
	Bay Hill
Sketches:	Sea Island
	Duke
	Innisbrook

Jim Fitzpatrick

Jim Fitzpatrick has always had a passion for art and golf. In his professional career he has been a course designer, teaching pro, and golf shop operator trying to find his niche. Fortunately, Jim combined both of his passions when he hit upon the idea of golf art. When his first two paintings sold within a week, he realized there was a demand for his unique work. Thus was launched the J. Fitzpatrick collection, introduced in 1985. Since then his work has earned worldwide acclaim, being featured in shops and galleries in Japan, Canada, and the United States. Golf greats Lee Trevino, Arnold Palmer, and Chi Chi Rodriguez collect his work.

Success has not come without effort. Hidden behind his easy-going, soft-spoken manner lie tremendous energy, foresight, and dedication to making a vision come true. Jim spends up to 300 hours - almost two months - to create a painting.

Many of his paintings have been produced for golf tournaments, clubs, and events such as the 1993 Tour Championship at the Olympic Club, the 1992 Ben Hogan Pebble Beach Invitational, the Inaugural LPGA Skins Game in 1990, the 1998 Senior Skins Game, and the Royal Canadian Golf Association's Canadian Open.

Jim's golf landscapes run so true to life that the golf hole portrayed is easily recognized by those who know the course and the artwork becomes a treasured momento. Jim's philosophy has always been to create a beautiful landscape where a golf hole got in the way.

Fitzpatrick's obvious delight in creating golf art reflects his own love for the game, which, combined with his talent, has made him an honored figure in the golf world.

The J. Fitzpatrick collection, including limited edition prints and custom framing, is available through:
JB Publishers (916) 624-1487.

CREDITS:

Paintings:	La Paloma
	Gray Hawk
	Pasatiempo
	Squaw Creek
	PGA West
	Mauna Lani
	Pumpkin Ridge
Sepia Tone:	Alister MacKenzie

Gordon Wheeler

Gordon Wheeler has developed his self-taught and highly personalized style with paintings full of vibrant color and realistic in detail. They include impressions gained first-hand through observation and close study of the subjects chosen. He evolved through oils, watercolors, and acrylics, working mainly in acrylics at this time.

During the painting of a series of commissioned watercolors for the state of South Carolina, he was encouraged to have some of his paintings reproduced as limited edition prints. Early success with the first prints led to a new career as a professional artist.

Gordon loves painting a variety of subjects including the breathtaking beauty of historic Charleston, where he resides with his wife Paula. He continues to expand his choice of subjects, inspired by diverse personal experiences and travels.

Gordon has loved golf for as long as he can remember. Living in a state blessed with hundreds of great courses and a climate permitting year-round play is a dream come true. Maintaining his studio at his home overlooking the ninth green next to the clubhouse enables Gordon to merge his two passions.

His first golf prints were of "Amen Corner" and the practice range at Augusta National Golf Course. Gordon achieved wide recognition when he was commissioned to paint the famed ocean course for the official 1991 Ryder Cup prints and posters. He has achieved a high degree of success with his golf art, which is collected worldwide. He has been called upon to paint many courses for various PGA events, including the 1991 and 1995 Ryder Cup, the 78th and 79th PGA Championship, the 1997 World Cup of Golf, the 80th PGA Championship, and the 1998 PGA Tour Championship.

Gordon's original paintings, limited edition prints, and posters are available through the Gordon Wheeler Gallery, 180 East Bay Street, Charleston, SC 29401. Phone: (843) 722-2546.

CREDITS:

Paintings: Wild Dunes

Ocean Course

TPC Scottsdale

Live Oak

Michael E. Ventola, Sr.

During his career, Mike has acted as a color consultant for many prestigious firms. He feels his greatest achievement has been his 35 years of service to The National Geographic Society. His accomplishments led to an appointment as Fine Arts Reproduction Consultant to the White House Historical Society during publication of the book "Nation's Pride."

CREDITS:

Paintings: Hartefeld

Dave Chapple

Dave Chapple's fascination with nature reaches back to his childhood experiences in the Sierra Mountains.

"My family had a cabin in the Sierras very near Yosemite, I was exposed to things as a child that hardly exist anywhere anymore. It was this early exposure to nature that piqued my interest and prepared me for a career in art."

At an early age, Chapple began drawing the subject that interested him most – the wildlife of the Sierras. Though he seemed destined to an art career, there was yet another profession in store for him. His college career allowed him to pursue his interest in nature. He worked part-time at the Santa Barbara Natural History Museum, where he acquired first-hand knowledge of anatomy as he perfected his taxidermy skills. His selection as an All-American football player while at the University of California at Santa Barbara allowed him to pursue his dream of a career in professional sports, a dream he realized in a five-year stint with the Los Angeles Rams. The highlight of his NFL career was the 1972 season. He led the league in punting, set an all-time record for the longest punt, and was named All-Pro for his performance.

Still, Chapple kept on with his first love – his art – continuing to refine and perfect his craft. Beginning in colored pencils and watercolor, he soon began exploring etching as a medium – a medium that especially suited his love of fine detail. Starting with simple one-color etchings, he eventually developed the full-color, finely crafted multi-plate etchings.

He developed a distinctive style of combining multi-stage etched images with hand-tinting. He has since expanded his artwork to include sculpture (both monumental and gallery edition pieces) and paintings of wildlife, landscape, and golf. He quickly established a rapidly growing following on his native West Coast. Now his paintings, bronzes, and etchings are praised and sought internationally by followers of fine art. Private collectors, sportsmen, galleries, and corporations are among the many who eagerly await the newest Chapple artwork. After leaving an impressive career in professional football, *Chapple has been able to create an equally impressive career in art in just a few years.*

CREDITS:

Paintings:	PGA National
	Troon North
	Pelican Hill
	Mauna Kea
	Desert Songbird
	Sailfish Watercolor
	Fishing Fleet
	Water Lilly/Basking Turtle
	Torrey Pines, Quail
	Troon North, Desert Quail
	Doves

Diane Selby

Diane has always had a passion for the arts. Armed with incredible talent and starting with a scholarship from the Atlanta School of Art, Diane's thirty year career has blossomed due to her skills in many mediums and use of diverse subject matter. Her involvement with Swanston Fine Art Gallery in Atlanta has led to sales and commissioned paintings that have been in demand by a large variety of corporate and private collectors.

Diane has been studying under the watchful eye of noted golf artist Linda Hartough, which has led her to her most recent venture into golf art.

For additional information on Diane's prints & paintings contact:

The Linda Hartough Gallery
PO Box 21325, Hilton Head Island, SC 29925
Tel: (843) 836-3821 FAX: (843) 836-3249
Toll Free: (888) 333-1525

CREDITS:

Paintings:	Furman University
	Osprey Cove
Sketches:	Furman University
	Osprey Cove

Bernie Fuchs

Bernie Fuchs has achieved a degree of recognition rarely experienced by a living artist. He was named Artist of the Year by the Artists Guild of New York before reaching the age of 30. He is the youngest artist ever selected to join the Society of Illustrators Hall of Fame, joining such notables as Norman Rockwell, Frederic Remington, and Winslow Homer. In 1991, he was named sports artist of the year by the United States Sports Academy.

His work has appeared in every major magazine from "The New Yorker" to "Golf Digest." He was commissioned to do a series of prints of the World Golf Hall of Fame, and several of his original oil paints will be on display there.

Golf is a familiar subject for Fuchs. His first assignment for "Sports Illustrated" 25 years ago was The Masters. His painting of Tony Jacklin hitting the key shot to win the U.S. Open at Hazeltine in 1970 made the "Sports Illustrated" cover, as did a dozen other sports subjects in the years following. Recently he painted a series for the Players Championship of the famous last three holes of TPC Sawgrass in Florida. A golfer himself, he lives and works in Westport, Connecticut.

CREDITS:

Painting: *Walter Hagen*

Sam Snead

Jimmy Demeret

Paul Milosevich

A 1996 West Texas Walk of Fame inductee, Paul Milosevich was born in Trinidad, Colorado. After receiving his Master of Arts degree at California State University, he moved to Odessa, Texas, to teach at Odessa College. In 1970, he moved to Lubbock, Texas, where he taught at Texas Tech University for the next five years. Although Paul Milosevich may be known best for his pencil sketches of Willie Nelson, Waylon Jennings, Tom T. Hall, and others, his artwork hangs in seven national museums, including the U.S. Golf Association, the Texas Golf Hall of Fame, the Pro Football Hall of Fame, the Nashville Songwriters' Hall of Fame, the Buick Museum, the Museum of the Southwest, and the Texas Tech Museum. His corporate clients include the Disney Corporation, RCA, MCA, Mercury Records, The Ben Hogan Company, Warner Brothers, and The World Golf Village.

Mr. Milosevich is the subject of a 30-year retrospective book, "Out of the Ordinary: The Art of Paul Milosevich," published by Texas Tech University Press. A subsequent book, "Texas Golf Legends," contains 100 portraits by Mr. Milosevich. His work has been featured in "Southwest Art Magazine," "NBC Today Show," "Texas Monthly," "Texas Country Reporter," "Golf World," "Golf Illustrated," and "Japan Golf."

CREDITS:

Painting: *Harvey Penick*

Golf Clubs Still Life

Legends of Course Design

Ball Washer

Don Patterson

Don Patterson is a nationally recognized watercolorist. He has exhibited in museums and galleries from coast to coast, Japan, and Canada. He is the recipient of awards from national juried exhibitions hosted by the following organizations: American Watercolor Society, The Salmagundi Club, National Watercolor Society, Philadelphia Water Color Club, Rhode Island Watercolor Society, Pennsylvania Watercolor Society, Pittsburgh Aqueous, The Arts Guild of Old Forge, Inc., The American Artists Professional League, Kentucky Watercolor Society, Texas Watercolor Society, Mississippi Watercolor Society, Western Colorado Center for the Arts, and San Diego Watercolor Society.

He has been elected to membership in the American Watercolor Society, the National Watercolor Society, Allied Artists of America, Audubon Artists, Inc., Knickerbocker Artists USA, the Pennsylvania Watercolor Society, and he has been a Board Member of the Philadelphia Water Color Club since 1982.

Patterson was featured in the December 1987 issue of "American Artists" magazine on PBS Television's "Outdoor Pennsylvania" in 1988. In 1990, he was selected a winner in "American Artists" competition, "Preserving Our Natural Resource." He was also featured in the December 1990 issue of "U.S. Art.". He was one of 90 top American watercolorists chosen for "Splash II" and "Splash IV," books published by North Light. He appeared in both Spring 1995 watercolor issues of "American Artists" and "The Artist's."

In 1997, his work was selected for the book "Best of Watercolor 2" by Rockport Publishers.

CREDITS:

Painting: Hershey

Sketch: Hershey

Paul Kuchno

Since his days as a caddy at the Sunset Country Club in St. Louis, his native city, Paul has loved the game of golf. His golf paintings combine his outstanding craft with an intense love of his subject matter. As a golfer, Paul captures the challenge of the scene, while he sees its beauty through the eyes of an artist.

Paul studied art at the American Academy of Art in Chicago, and he studied watercolor under Irving Shapiro. He has taught watercolor at the Art Student's League in San Juan, Puerto Rico, and was the tournament artist for the GTE Classic in Tampa, Florida, for seven years. Kuchno is also a signature member of the Florida Watercolor Society.

Internationally known for his golf art, his paintings have been published in numerous limited editions. His art is well-represented in collections of major corporations and treasured by many private collectors.

For additional information on Mr. Kuchno's work, please contact:

Kuchno Watercolors

15001 Naples Place, Tampa, FL 33624

(813) 264-6452

Email: kuchno@gte.net

CREDITS:

Paintings: World Woods

St. Ives

The Hermitage

Sketches: St. Ives

Jesse Hyde

Jesse Hyde is a free-lance artist and golf enthusiast specializing in golf course landscape art and illustration since 1985. Jesse studied art a Carnegie-Mellon University in Pittsburgh, Pennsylvania and received his Bachelor's degree before doing graduate work at the Indiana University of Pennsylvania.

Jesse has painted many notable courses in the Northeast like Merion and Muirfield Village. Accolades include publication of Mr. Hyde's illustrations of the Chicago sports scene in the 1990 U.S. Open Tournament program at Medinah. In the same year, Jesse's aerial painting of the Poppy Hill Golf Club was featured in the Pebble Beach Pro-Am Tournament program.

Recently Jesse was chosen as the featured artist at the 1994 Men's U.S. Open at the Oakmont Country Club. He was also a commissioned artist for the 1993 Men's U.S. Open held at Baltusrol. These tournaments featured original artwork, as well as limited edition lithograph prints for purchase.

Jesse has been named several times to "Who's Who Among America's Teachers" and was named 1996 Oswayo Valley Alumni Association's Teacher of the Year (Shinglehouse, PA). He has appeared as the celebrity guest during the July 5, 1996, television broadcast of a Pittsburgh Pirates baseball game and has also displayed a painting of Machrihanish Golf Club in Scotland at the 1997 U.S. Open. Commissioned projects include a painting of Fred Couples' victory at the Masters for the 1995 Family House Golf Tournament Auction, Pittsburgh; a landscape for a private hunting/fishing lodge in Alaska; and a painting of Loch Lomond Golf Club, Scotland, for a private collector.

Originally from the Pittsburgh area, Jesse's studio is located in Shinglehouse, Pennsylvania, where he resides with his wife and two sons. Mr. Hyde's services are available to individuals, clubs, and organizations on a commission or consignment basis. Contact Jesse at (814) 697-7239.

CREDITS:
Painting: Hartefeld National
Sketch: Hartefeld National

Tom Lynch

When you look at Tom Lynch's paintings, be prepared to surrender your imagination to an exciting world of shimmering color and exciting mood. Characterized by a romantic quality of unusual and dramatic lighting, each painting is infused with a feeling for the passing of time and the evanescence of the moment.

Whether his subjects be of the secluded north woods, the sun-drenched arid desert, windswept palms in the South, a turbulent sky, or serene lake, Tom Lynch knows how to capture that essence on paper.

"My challenge is to have the viewer first notice the beauty of the landscape and then notice that it is a golf course second. The golf course is a natural for a work of art."

He adds, "I emphasize the changes the architect has created or embellished, and use my artistic skills to capture the beauty of light and color. All the parts are there, but how I highlight and balance with color, or bring out the shadows is the final touch, the final complement to what is a beautiful scene." This skill has brought much acclaim to Arlington Heights, Illinois, artist Tom Lynch: His work has been featured at the last four U.S. Opens. He has completed art for major developers, designers, tour players, and an impressive list of private clubs.

"People are beginning to realize that a painting of a golf course is a viable form of art, and not whimsical or casual," Lynch asserts. "It's coming into vogue and gaining an importance. It's not trendy. It's an established form of art to be looking at, appreciated, and collected." Contact Tom Lynch at (630) 851-2652.

CREDITS:
Paintings: World Woods
              Cog Hill
              Cantigny

George T. Lawrence, Jr.

For many years George Lawrence felt equally at home on a great golf course or in a world-class museum, but he did not combine his two passions until 1989 when approached by his golf club, Westhampton Country Club on Long Island, to create two large golf scenes in oil to commemorate the club's centennial celebrations.

A typical commissioned golf landscape requires Lawrence to make several visits to the course for early morning and late afternoon photo sessions. He does this to ensure that critical features, as well as subtle nuances, are caught in the best light.

Lawrence's golf scenes have a remarkably true-to-life quality to them. Standing in front on one of his works, golfers can almost sense the air temperature and time of day. Creating this effect is the result of a skilled technique, a practiced eye, and plain hard work. Sunrise sightings of him patiently perched, heron-like, on a ladder are often reported by grounds crews.

At about the time he designed his first 18-hole golf course at the age of 16, Lawrence's handicap dropped to four, and for the last 30 years it has gotten as low as one and never higher than five. His passion for and knowledge of the game are very evident in his paintings.

Until recently, Lawrence largely confined his work to the New York Metropolitan area. However, in addition to scenes of courses in the South, West, and Midwest, he has created several paintings of golf courses in Ireland, a familiar and favorite place to visit.

The windswept east end of Long Island is home to some of the world's finest golf courses, most notably Shinnecock Hills, The Maidstone Club, The National Golf Links, and Rees Jones' new Atlantic Golf Club. It is there that Lawrence has honed his artistic skills. His commissioned works include several oils of each of these magnificent layouts. Contact the Scottsdale Collection at (301) 765-0074.

CREDITS:

Painting: Bethpage

Sketch: Bethpage

William Mangum

William Mangum has created over 1,200 original watercolor paintings of magnificent places all over the world in his 20-year career as an artist. He has reproduced nearly 80 of those paintings as limited edition prints. Over 50 of those prints are sold out and enjoy an active secondary market.

The artist has owned and operated Carey-Mangum Gallery in the Lawndale Shopping Center in Greensboro since 1982. The gallery features the artist's original watercolors and limited edition prints and posters. Recently Mangum has added the extraordinary figurative sculptures of artist Richard MacDonald to his gallery. William Mangum's prints are available in over 200 galleries nationwide. As the publisher and distributor of his own artwork, William limits the size of his editions, thus ensuring the quality and integrity of his products.

Although the artist is primarily known for his scenes of North Carolina, most of Mangum's original paintings depict international subjects. He has travelled to Bermuda, Austria, Switzerland, England, Greece, and Italy to capture the beauty found in different parts of the world.

On three separate occasions, the Greater Greensboro Open Golf Tournament commissioned William Mangum to create images featured in their sponsorship packages and promotional materials. Recently the 1996 Women's Open at Pine Needles Lodge and Golf Club in Pinehurst was commemorated by the artist.

The artist is a graduate with a Bachelor of Fine Arts and Master of Fine Arts from the University of North Carolina at Greensboro. His professional affiliations include the North Carolina Watercolor Society, the Southern Watercolor Society, and associate memberships with the American Watercolor and National Watercolor Societies, and the Society of Illustrators.

CREDITS:

Painting: Pine Needles

Matt Scharlé

Matt Scharlé works full-time as an artist for The Franklin Mint, where he manages the computer-design department. His job deals with all aspects of digital design from high resolution retouching to illustration to 3-D design and animation. Despite his busy schedule, he still manages to find time to paint the traditional way.

"I love to paint with a real brush and paint because the results are much more rewarding and the paintings have a lot more subtle detail than I can achieve with a computer-generated image."

He started his career painting wildlife in the mid 1980s. Focusing mainly on fish and ducks, Matt painted the 1993 New Jersey trout stamp and won the 1995 New Hampshire duck stamp. He was also chosen to be the New Jersey Ducks Unlimited sponsor artist for 1994. One can't help but notice the tremendous detail in Matt's landscapes. Golf courses seem to have been a natural evolution of his inspirations.

"My favorite images are the ones that contrast the beautifully manicured gardens against the wild wetlands. That tempting invitation to escape the boundaries of the status quo. As a kid I loved when my foot slipped off the bank into the creek. I try to capture that 'one wet foot' feeling in my paintings. I want the viewer to say, 'I've been there' when they see my paintings.

"In my wildlife paintings I feel it's important to show the viewer the subject's natural environment that is where this creature lives. Now I'd like to show you where the animal called the golfer lives along with some of my old friends."

Matt Scharlé - 16 Beaver Drive, Barrington, NJ 08007
(609) 546-7548

CREDITS:

Paintings:	Little River
	Seaview
	Reynolds Plantation
	Chateau Elan Woodlands
	Diablo Grande
Sketches:	Little River

Elizabeth Peper

Elizabeth (Libby) White grew up in Kansas City, Missouri. She attended college in Saratoga Springs, New York, majoring in studio art. First employed as a commercial artist in the advertising field, she gained technical expertise and precision skills. Libby met George Peper (now Editor-in-Chief, of "Golf Magazine") whom she married in 1978.

Sotheby's (the world-famous auction house) hired Libby to aid in art appraisal, which rekindled her interest in painting. In 1986, George collaborated with Libby, utilizing her illustrations for the book "Golf Courses of the PGA Tour" and the book "Grand Slam of Golf in 1990." Since illustrating her first book, Libby has become recognized internationally as a premier golf artist, known for her technical accuracy and amazing 3-D depth.

Elizabeth Peper's credits and contributions include painting topographic images and course maps for the following publications, tournaments, organizations, and individuals: The U.S. Open, The British Open, The Masters, The Ryder Cup, the PGA Tour, and the USGA.

Among Libby's other projects the Dream Course consists of 18 images which began when the owners of Northstar were gathering research material for a line of golf art. They came upon a book written by George Peper with illustrations by Libby. She was commissioned to produce one painting.

Libby's work is 3-D, it comes alive. When she paints an ocean you not only see it, you smell it – unexpectedly, you are transported there to feel the breeze, select your club, and plan your shot.

For any information on Libby's work, please contact:
Northstar Art & Mirror, Inc.
2828 Hedberg Drive, Minnetonka, MN 55305
(612) 593-5525

CREDITS:

| Paintings: | Mauna Kea |
| | Cog Hill |

Noble Powell, III

An artist's world is a special place where emotions coexist with the realities of life. When this manifests itself on paper or canvas, we are given a personal invitation by the artist to share the experience. Fortunately, Noble Powell's world includes golf.

Drawing on his love for the "The Game," his appreciation for nature's landscapes, and his unparalleled sense of color and design, Noble creates dramatic paintings of the most famous golf landscapes in the world. One of the most intriguing aspects of his style is the manner in which Powell draws viewers into the scene, making them feel that they are an integral part of the setting.

His limited edition prints and commissioned original paintings have been enthusiastically received in Europe, Japan, Australia, as well as the United States. He has received numerous national and regional awards, and his "One Man Shows" have earned him a dedicated following by those who appreciate a consummate artistan. Noble Powell, III, has become one of the most recognized names in the world of sports art today.

Noble was commissioned by the Pebble Beach Company to create a series of images of the world-famous Pebble Beach Golf Links, as well as the Links at Spanish Bay. This print series was the first of its kind authorized and licensed by the Pebble Beach Company. Mr. Powell has also produced a print series of the Augusta National Golf Club, site of the annual Masters Tournament. His work also includes renderings of recent British Open venues – Turnberry in 1994 and St. Andrews in 1995. He has just completed a series of original paintings for Pinehurst, site of the 1999 U.S. Open.

Mr. Powell has been painting professionally for 25 years. Born and raised in California, he received his Bachelor of Fine Arts degree from the Santa Barbara Art Institute, a Masters in Fine Arts from California State University (Long Beach), and a Certificate in Commercial Art from the University of California at Santa Barbara.

Noble maintains his studio and his home in Camarillo, California, where he lives with this wife and three children. Mr. Powell is represented and published by Cypress Classics of Pebble Beach, California.

CREDITS:

Paintings: Pinehurst
                     Spanish Bay

W. D. Wood

W. D. Wood is a self-taught watercolorist and muralist. Wintergreen is his first entry into golf art.

His works hang in private and corporate collections, including Genicom and Duracell corporations. Wood's murals adorn the walls of many private and historic homes in Virginia, including Montebello, birthplace of Zachary Taylor.

His work is offered to the interior design trade in Washington, D.C., and Atlanta. His works are being shown at Bryant Studio Gallery, Bryant, Virginia, The Second Street Gallery, Charlottesville, Virginia, and Stedman House of Wintergreen, Wintergreen, Virginia.

CREDITS:

Paintings: Wintergreen

Alexander Kalinin

"If there is one constant in life, it is change." Alexander Kalinin's life has offered him the excitement and challenge of change from his early years in Yugoslavia, art education in England, migration to Canada, and in 1975 to Beaufort, South Carolina. Since 1981 Kalinin has maintained his studios in a lovely century-old Victorian home with his wife Anne at the Anne Tutt Gallery in Macon, Georgia's, Historic District and at Pine Mountain, Georgia, near Callaway Gardens.

This artist's masterful handling of light and color and his romantic approach to his subjects have led him to be chosen for many corporate and private collections.

Alexander Kalinin has adopted Georgia and the South, warmly embracing their tremendous variety of land and seascapes as subjects for his paintings. The Kalinins also travel through the United States and abroad to research exciting new subjects for his work. *"I've discovered inspiration as near as your own back garden and constantly at Georgia's beautiful Callaway Gardens and as far as Pateley Bridge, Yorkshire, or the fabulous Hawaiian and California golf courses. One needs an eternity and then some to paint his inspirations!"*

A growing collection of Kalinin's Fine Art Collector prints includes vibrant landscapes of Callaway Gardens, North Georgia mountain subjects, peach orchards, and so on. A new edition is a handsome poster and also a limited edition print entitled *"Day Butterfly Center, Callaway Gardens,"* plus *"A Taste of Summer,"* a butterfly sipping nectar in a field of cleome, and an inviting sunlit walk, *"Azalea Pathway."*

Kalinin is equally comfortable with watercolor, oil, pastel, and acrylic. *"I make a choice of the media that will best create the mood I feel for the painting."*

CREDITS

Paintings	Callaway Gardens
	Sugarloaf
Pencil sketches:	Callaway Gardens

A. J. Rudisill

The realism of living among his subjects, from the age of 14 on, when the Rudisill family moved from Philadelphia to the coastal region of the South Jersey shores, propelled young A. J. Rudisill into a career of painting wildlife.

Living, walking, and fully submerging himself into the environment of the marshes of his new-found home, Mr. Rudisill's brilliant sensitivities to his subject - birds, fishes, waterfowl (he is an avid fisherman, too) and terrain - launched him on an art career that was entirely self-taught. Mastering pen and brush, his observation and attention to a flutter or wings spread in flight, as expressed by many of his fellow sportsmen who have accompanied him on his explorations through the fields and marshlands, indicate the preciseness of the illustrative studies of his many subjects.

In choosing to paint the elements of nature, Mr. Rudisill has surrounded himself with one of America's foremost wildlife refugees - the South Jersey area - a habitat for migrating water fowl and birds, spread over thousands of square miles. And in quest of his prey, to be recorded by pencil and pad and refined in watercolors exacting the beauty of the elements, he has continued his trek to bring his many paintings where they rightfully belong, in the forefront of American art.

CREDITS:

Paintings:	Chateau Elan, Legends
	Blue Heron Pines
Sketches:	Chateau Elan
Sculpture:	Blue Heron Pines

Graeme Baxter

Graeme Baxter is one of the world's most highly acclaimed painters of golfing landscapes. His work is admired and prized internationally for its superb quality, depth of feeling, and knowledge of the subject. His paintings hang in famous clubhouses as far afield as the Honourable Company of Edinburgh Golfers at Muirfield, Scotland, and Augusta National, home of the U. S. Masters.

Graeme Baxter was born in Scotland, cradle of this royal and ancient game. In his paintings of golfing landscapes, he works with a passion and inner certainty that Scots bring in such measures to the game they invented and love.

Graeme Baxter is artist to the PGA, the European Tour and, since 1991, he has been the official artist to the Ryder Cup. A recent appointment is official artist for the President's Cup, the 1998 tournament being played in Melbourne, Australia. In addition, his appointment as artist for the 25th Anniversary of the Dunlop Phoenix Tournament in Japan and several other important commissions in Australia, Indonesia, and other Far Eastern countries have further enlarged his reputation and ensure that the Baxter Print Collection of limited and open edition golf prints remains the most comprehensive in the world today.

CREDITS:

Painting: Pebble Beach
*   Ocean Course*

Kenneth Reed, F.R.S.A.

Born in Hexham, Northumberland, Kenneth Reed studied at Newcastle College of Art & Design and became a Fellow of the Royal Society of Arts (FRSA) in 1962. He is a member of the British Golf Collectors' Society and possesses an intimate knowledge of the game, borne out by his continuous attendance at the British Open Championship since 1968.

During the 1960s, on completion of his studies, he practiced graphic design with an international packaging company and later as a free-lance designer and illustrator.

From 1969 on, he lectured at Cleveland College of Art & Design, combining his special commission paintings with his lectures until 1996 when international demand for his work required him to dedicate his skills full-time.

This demand was the result of joining with Old Troon Sporting Antiques, who became managing agents. Commissions on an annual basis are in place with The Royal and Ancient Golf Club of St. Andrews, the USGA of America, and the U.S. Women's Open, to mention but a few.

Some of Kenneth's clients are the Golf Hall of Fame, Pinehurst National, Royal Troon, the USGA, Royal and Ancient G.C. St. Andrews, and "The Wall Street Journal."

"Reed is more than a rigid realist. While others use their paint brushes to slavishly copy photographs, Reed goes the extra mile. His distinctive watercolors are as evocative as they are accurate. Anyone who has seen his St. Andrews skies knows that Ken takes the best of Mother Nature and then makes it even better." George F. Peper, Editor-in-Chief, "Golf Magazine."

Old Troon Sporting Antiques, 49 Ayr Street, Troon, Ayrshire KA106EB Scotland
(01144) 1292 311822

CREDITS:
Painting: Pine Needles
Sketch   Judy Bell

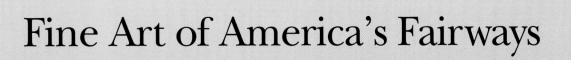

Fine Art of America's Fairways

West

7th Hole
By Linda Hartough

Pebble Beach

PEBBLE BEACH, CA

There may not be enough superlatives in the English language to adequately describe Pebble Beach. Its ocean scenery is renowned. It boasts swaying beach grass, pristine white sand, and fragrant pines, and broad-crowned cypress trees can be found edging the clipped greens along the windswept shoreline. There is deep sapphire water working itself into a salty froth, hurling its giant breakers into craggy granite cliffs. There is no denying that Pebble Beach has a spectacular setting and a most challenging course. Jack Nicklaus, arguably the greatest golfer of all time, was moved to say, "If I had only one more round to play, I would choose to play it at Pebble Beach. I have loved this course from the first time I saw it."

Monterey Peninsula, shaped by volcanic and perhaps mystic forces along the eastern rim of northern California, provided a rich medium on which to carve this golf course – a course widely considered to be one of the best in the world. It offers a temperate climate, a lush collection of plant life, a varied range of terrain, and extraordinary natural beauty.

In 1602, Spanish explorer Sebastian Vizcaino found the safe harbor of Monterey Bay, noting it in his logs and performing a ritual of possession for his country. By 1770, the Franciscans established the Mission San Carlos and made it the seat of Spanish authority in California. Later,

when Mexico threw off Spanish rule, the area flew the flag of the Mexican Empire. In 1846, the United States extended its holdings, claiming Monterey as a prize after victory in the Mexican-American War. In 1850, California became the nation's 31st state and Monterey was its hub. However, this changed rapidly with the discovery of gold near Sacramento.

Monterey represented a different kind of gold. It was an escape from the dirty rough- and-tumble gold rush cities to the soft luxury of refreshing landscape. In 1879, rail lines arrived and in 1880 the Hotel Del Monte was built. Monterey was now poised to become a fabulous destination for the booming resort industry.

It was 1897 before golf would become part of the picture. The Del Monte Golf Course was primitive, even by the standards of the day. Its design exhibited no respect for the sweeping natural contours of the land; instead, it seemed to have been laid out with a ruler. Its fairways were barren, its greens were little more than scraped-away dunes, its bunkers were arranged in straight lines, its hazards appeared to be a pocketful of chocolate kisses dropped in neat rows mostly to the right.

A new layout was needed to compete with and surpass the quality of golf courses springing up in the mountains along the eastern seaboard. There, professionals like

18th Hole
By Graeme Baxter

17th Hole
By Linda Hartough

Donald Ross were raising the standards of golf course design to an art. At Pebble Beach, however, an amateur was chosen for the honors. He was Jack Neville, five-time winner of the California State Amateurs and a member of the winning 1923 U.S. Walker Cup team.

Planning for the new golf course began in 1913, but construction had to wait until World War I ended. There were few professional golf course architects at the time, so Neville assembled his team from a group of other talented, knowledgeable amateurs, including California amateur champion Douglas Grant. It is a credit to Neville and Grant that their understanding of and love for the game influenced their decision to transform Pebble Beach into one of the most challenging and beloved courses in the world.

Neville recognized the potential of mixing golf with a beautiful environment. The primary attraction was the ocean. He challenged himself to place as many holes along the shore of Carmel Bay. A straightforward figure-eight design put more than half the course along the cliffs, where it flowed naturally back to the 18th hole, which many have described as the best finishing hole in golf. The course opened in 1919.

The formidable reputation of Pebble Beach spread fast. In 1929, it hosted the U.S. Amateur Championship. In subsequent years it would host the U.S. Women's Amateur, the PGA, and three U.S. Opens, taking on the status of an extraordinary golf course, globally recognized for its outstanding level of play and breathtaking setting.

Probably most famous among its events was the Bing Crosby National Pro-Am, in which celebrities were paired

5th Hole - Spanish Bay
By Noble Powell

with golfers for the benefit of charity. The Crosby Clambake became an American institution, and the stunning beauty of Pebble Beach became part of the American landscape. It was beamed into televisions all over the world. Hollywood was smitten with Monterey and the beauty that was so ingeniously preserved and utilized at Pebble Beach. Several films were shot on location there, including "National Velvet."

Decent scores here demand that a golfer bring advance planning to the tee, as Jack Nicklaus discovered when he played Pebble Beach to win his second U.S. Amateur Championship. Knowing the course and planning his approach put him in great shape. Even his nemesis, the second hole, succumbed to Nicklaus' strategy.

Nicklaus was painfully aware that trouble lay in store for anyone who misjudged the hidden dangers of Number Two. "I like the second at Pebble very much, perhaps because it looks like such a pushover but can destroy you unless you handle it with care," he said. That awareness, which was an outgrowth of sometimes painful experiences, helped Nicklaus become the only man to win the U.S. Amateur (1961) and the U.S. Open (1972) on the same golf course. He also won three Bing Crosby titles at Pebble Beach.

The difficulty of Pebble Beach is perhaps best outlined by its golf pro, Johnny Miller. He calls Number One a "sneaky hole because if you do not drive in the fairway, all kinds of problems await you." Of Numbers Three and Four, he uses the power of understatement when he says, "There are a lot of problems here." Number Five he calls "a terrifying hole for the average player. All kinds of problems

await you if you miss the fairway on Number Six" – this is the hole where many golfers believe the game really begins. Number Seven, "probably one of the most photographed holes in the world, has an ever-changing personality that depends on the wind and makes it a fantastic little hole." What happens after Number Seven, Miller says, "is full of horror stories."

Number Eight is "maybe the most dramatic and dangerous par four in all of golf," says Miller, finishing uphill from a blind tee shot. Number Nine is longer and "requires a heroic second shot." Number Ten "features beautiful views of the ocean, Point Lobos, the beautiful white sands of Carmel Beach, and the most difficult tee shot on the course. Together, these three are acknowledged to be the hardest par fours in a row in the world." Miller says these are the holes that all of a sudden can bite your round big-time.

Tiny greens, predatory traps, menacing bunkers, deadly barrancas, and silver-like fairways require accuracy because at Pebble Beach, it is disaster to get behind. The course grows in difficulty with each hole, and every shot counts.

Neville's vision was to create an understated course that flowed naturally with the terrain and revealed the unequaled vistas of its coastal location. While he was at it, he set up a treacherous mine field – a layout where the potential for disintegration is ever present.

So carefully did Neville plan his course, it has remained basically unchanged during the nearly 80 years since it opened. It has, in fact, become the pinnacle of achievement for amateur and professional golfers alike.

9th Hole - Fazio
By Adriano Manocchia

Barton Creek

AUSTIN, TX

Nestled within 4,800 acres of scenic Texas Hill Country in Austin lies Barton Creek Resort, proudly recognized as one of the premier golfing destinations in the country. The resort's three championship golf courses are a tribute to both the game and the unique terrain of the Hill Country, rightfully earning Barton Creek that distinction.

People come to Barton Creek for golf. The trio of courses was designed by masters of modern day golf course architecture - Tom Fazio, Arnold Palmer, Ben Crenshaw and partner, Bill Coore. With such talent in one location, it is easy to see why Barton Creek holds so much attraction for so many golfers.

Barton Creek's signature golf course is an astonishingly beautiful design masterpiece by Tom Fazio. The architectural layout features dramatic cliff-lined fairways, natural limestone caves, waterfalls, and superb Penncross bent grass greens which give golfers 18 holes of pure pleasure with no shortage of challenge. The visual impact created by significant elevation changes contributes to making this an unforgettable golfing experience for everyone.

Fazio puts a premium on long accurate drives. Small undulating greens and grass bunkers make for a shotmaker's paradise. Six different sets of tee boxes offer a comfortable choice for players of all skill levels.

Established in 1986, the Fazio Course quickly amassed accolades. "Golf Digest" has ranked it among the Best Resort Courses in America, the number two course in Texas, and perhaps most impressively, 60th on the revered list of the 100 Greatest Golf Courses in America. The course is consistently named Overall Favorite by Texas Professional Golfers and carries the distinction of not only having one of its holes, the 18th, listed among the Most Difficult Golf Holes, but also having several holes listed among the State's 18 Best or Most Beautiful, namely the ninth, tenth, 16th and 18th, as rated by "The Dallas Morning News."

With so many great reviews and spectacular holes, the Fazio Course was a natural selection to host the Liberty Mutual Legends of Golf Senior Tournament, and remained the home of the tournament from 1990 to 1994. This course is stunning, and it ranks among the favorites of golf experts and enthusiasts everywhere.

Ben Crenshaw, Austin's well-known native son and Barton Creek's own touring professional, was taken with the natural beauty of the Texas Hill Country, and he and partner Bill Coore focused their attention on using the land's resplendent qualities in the design of their course. Rolling hills, natural plateaus, soft contours, and native vegetation are harmoniously woven into a playable championship layout, providing a variety of interesting holes that will delight both amateur and well-traveled golfers.

Crenshaw admits his is an "old style" philosophy. "We believe the best architect is nature and the best players' courses make good use of the natural terrain," explained Crenshaw. "We let the land dictate the routing rather than imposing ourselves on the landscape."

As an ardent student of golf's history, Crenshaw offers a rare taste of a traditional layout in his design. The course features broad rolling fairways and widely varied green sizes, and is a fitting tribute to the way the game was once played. The large, undulating putting surfaces give golfers their biggest challenge. While the average golfer will attempt to use the natural slopes to aid an approach shot, the low handicap player faces the challenge of positioning the ball at the most advantageous point for an approach putt.

Durable grasses were utilized as part of the environmentally sensitive considerations. Keeping in mind the heat and drought conditions that affect the area, Bermuda 419 was used on the fairways and Tidwarf Bermuda was laid on the greens.

The 18th hole is an exciting climax which plays slightly uphill. Approach shots must cross a running creek to land on a low-lying green, which is seemingly etched into the hillside. The Crenshaw and Coore Course is both forgiving for the novice and challenging for the seasoned golfer.

Barton Creek's third course, the Lakeside, is a hidden retreat perched on a secluded hilltop overlooking Lake Travis, to the west of the resort's main facility. Designed by the King of Golf, Arnold Palmer, the extraordinary Lakeside championship golf course opened for play in 1986. Striking panoramic lake views and twilight glimpses of white-tail deer offer a magnificent setting in which to play.

Prowess with a driver is a plus for a good round of golf here, as Palmer's course is a big-hitter's delight. The par-five 12th hole and par-four 13th hole are both doglegs left with sloping fairways that reward any player who can "turn the ball over and take it deep." Lakeside's signature 11th hole features a cascading waterfall and native flora, prompting "The Dallas Morning News" to rank the magnificent par-three among the 18 Most Beautiful in Texas. Professional golfers rate Palmer's design among the Top Ten Texas courses and consider Lakeside to have the best bent grass greens in the state. Guests can enjoy the quiet refuge of the clubhouse, which affords a lake view that is nothing short of fantastic.

Barton Creek is an exceptional resort for golf and has won several awards, including the distinguished Gold Tee and Gold Key awards by "Meeting & Conventions" magazine, as well as Successful Meetings Ace Award for Excellence in Golf and Meeting Facilities. "Conde Nast Traveler" named Barton Creek one of the Best Places to Stay in the World to Play Golf. Anyone who has been there will agree. A magnificent setting, the unsurpassed talents of some of the best architects in the business, three incredible courses ... Barton Creek has it all.

16th Hole - Talon
By Jim Fitzpatrick

"All of my artistic senses came to life when I came upon this scene.
The background is Pinnacle Peak, Scottsdales most distinguishing landmark.
The green settings with the long afternoon shadows were very dramatic, the pot
bunker is great golf achitecture and the two saguaro cacti standing sentinal
framed the scene perfectly."   *Artist Jim Fitzpatrick*

Grayhawk
Scottsdale, AZ

18th Hole - Raptor
By Val Longmore

Nothing about Scottsdale's renowned Grayhawk Golf Club is what you'd call "typical." For starters, Grayhawk is one of the most upscale golf courses available to the public, yet its attitude is decidedly "come as you are." It is golf the way you want it - which just so happens to be the Grayhawk family's unofficial, official motto.

Welcoming and inviting, Grayhawk feels like your second home. The staff is extremely efficient and friendly, the kind of folks you wouldn't mind swapping stories with after a round. They really go out of their way to make you comfortable. In fact, a lot of people who are household names (entertainers, sports figures, captains of industry, and the like) make regular stops at Grayhawk knowing that once they arrive, they can be themselves and have a good time, and no one is going to care who they are.

Two local guys who have come to like Grayhawk so much that they've signed on to be unofficial "ambassadors" for the club during their travels are PGA Tour standouts Phil Mickelson and Howard Twitty. Two other famed ambassadors are CBS golf commentators Peter Kostis and

Gary McCord. This dynamic duo of golf actually run the learning center at Grayhawk, providing their own brand of off-beat, but effective, golf instruction.

It is Grayhawk's two exceptional golf courses that provide beauty and drama to the locale. Talon, designed by former U. S. Open and PGA Champion David Graham and architect Gary Panks, easily ranks among the most exciting and dramatic golf courses ever built in the Southwest. It opened to a chorus of cheers in December 1994, and was immediately included on the list of the Top 10 You Can Play by "Golf Magazine." Since that time it has continued to accumulate industry accolades and honors at an impressive clip.

From its vantage point in the high Sonoran Desert, the 7,001-yard par 72 Talon Course provides panoramic views of the nearby McDowell Mountains, as well as the downtown Scottsdale and Phoenix skylines. But its true beauty lies in the way Talon has blended itself with the lush desert landscape.

The course opens with one of the most inspiring holes you will find anywhere. Named "Farrview," Talon's 428-yard par four first hole is dedicated to the late LPGA star and local hero, Heather Farr. A dear friend to the Grayhawk family and the first Grayhawk ambassador, she represented the golf club on the LPGA Tour until illness overtook her. Farrview features a stirring life-sized bronze of Heather, captured in her follow-through with her eyes staring down the fairway, watching for a ball that, like her spirit, will never fall to earth.

The poignancy of that monument may even help calm your first tee jitters. The hole, long and straight, provides a fairly gentle beginning to the round. In fact, all of the holes on Talon's front nine are like that. Interesting and fun, they give you quality play and pretty views without much intimidation.

However, as you make the turn, be prepared for the back nine, where every hole has the potential to deliver a knockout punch. Carved around a series of deep box canyons and dry desert washes, many of these holes invite players to flirt with the prospect of gutsy shots over deep ravines in hopes of earning an easy birdie or eagle as a reward. But like most things in the desert, these holes can bite. And they often have devoured players who underestimated the dangers they pose.

Of all the stunning holes on the back nine, three that typify the course are Swinging Bridge, Heaven or Hell, and Five Falls. Swinging Bridge, the par three, 175-yard 11th hole, features a rope bridge that leads to an island tee

Winning Putt
By Val Longmore

perched in the midst of the box canyon. The tee shot must carry all the way to the green...accurately. Thanks to some tricky bunkering and a severely sloping green, anything short or long is probable death. Lucky number 13, Heaven or Hell, is pure temptation. Only 303 yards from the back tees, short for a par four, it appears at first glance that a good tee shot over a 50-foot deep section of canyon will bring a low score reward. Don't be fooled by this devil's play, or you are likely to earn a few extra penance strokes, due to deceiving angles, large bunkers, and a tricky green. The 18th hole, Five Falls, is a massive 585-yard par five that seems to go on forever. Uphill, water, sand, and desert make the beautiful five level waterfall that flows behind the green an even sweeter oasis. Complementing Talon is Grayhawk's newest golf course, Raptor. Designed by famed architect Tom Fazio, Raptor is a true player's course, reminiscent of the classic designs of the old masters like Donald Ross and Allister Mackenzie. It was the first Fazio design in Arizona open for public play. If Talon provides Grayhawk's flash and sizzle, Raptor provides its soul. The 7,108-yard par 72 course meanders over gentle hills and across deep arroyos that are typical of the Sonoran Desert. Raptor features panoramic views of the nearby McDowell Mountains and skirts thick stands of giant saguaro cactus, palo verdes, ironwoods, and mesquite trees that were preserved when landscaping the course.

Typical of Raptor's challenge is its eighth hole, a 165-yard, par three named Aces & Eights. From the tee, this hole plays slightly downhill to a partially hidden green nestled in a natural amphitheater. Three large bunkers protect the front of the green and are strategically placed to fool the player into thinking the green is closer than it really is.

Another of Raptor's tough par threes is the 16th, a gem named Little Creek. It too plays downhill from the tee, and it's all carry to a green fronted by a pond and a bunker.

Of course, not all of Raptor's tests are short. The aptly named 11th, Sunset Grill, plays 572 yards directly into the setting sun. Fazio saved the best for last, though, with the 521-yard 18th, called Big Sky. With a 50-foot drop from tee to green, this hole offers diverse views of the mountains, the Valley and, of course, the big Arizona sky.

Raptor, like Talon, was named to the Top 100 You Can Play in the U.S. by "Golf Magazine" and is among the highest rated golf clubs in the Southwest. With two great courses and an impressive clubhouse, it is no surprise that Grayhawk has been home to a number of high profile golf events. The club has played host to the semi-finals and finals of the acclaimed Andersen Consulting World Championship of Golf, a unique match-play tournament that features many of the world's top players and gave birth to the new World Tour. Grayhawk has hosted numerous other prestigious golf tournaments, including several Phoenix Open Pro-Ams, the Heather Farr Trophy Matches, The Goldwater Cup Matches, the Southwest Amateur, and the Arizona State Amateur Championships.

Stunning, dramatic, and challenging, Grayhawk offers an enticing golf venue with a lure and appeal that can only be found in a special location. While demanding and not very forgiving, the rewards of playing these courses far outweigh any regrets brought on by overconfident swings. Surrounded by the alluring beauty of desert courses and the satisfaction that comes from tackling a challenge, any golfer could easily become yet another ambassador for the courses of Grayhawk.

Heather Farr Memorial
By Jerry Cox

Tamarron
DURANGO, CO

Nature began sculpting the setting for golf architect Arthur Hills'. Cliffs Golf Course at the Sheraton Tamarron Resort in Durango, Colorado, 65 million years ago when the San Juan mountain range was formed from rare continental volcanic eruptions. The finishing touches were applied by glacial ice caps that receded from the mountaintops two million years ago and wedged their way between the hillsides, leaving canyons that would one day be transformed into fairways.

The end result is Hills' 1974 "mountain masterpiece," as acclaimed by "Golf Digest" magazine, that gave rise to a whole genre of ski and golf resorts throughout this western state's extreme mountainous regions.

Located in the four corners section of Colorado where the state merges with Utah, New Mexico, and Arizona, the Sheraton Tamarron has prospered from its image as a remote mountain resort some 7,600 feet in the air, where activities other than golf and skiing include pursuits like horseback riding and river-rafting.

The Sheraton Resort Company acquired Tamarron in September of 1998, and leases the management of the Cliffs course to the Troon Golf Company Access to Durango is

1st Hole
By James Ross

mostly limited to one hour commuter flights from Denver, Phoenix, or Albuquerque, but that only adds to the charm of this former pioneering outpost.

The first pioneers willing to settle here were Pueblo and Ute Indian tribes. By the 16th century, Spanish explorers had charted the region, but it wasn't until the gold rush of the 1880s that the town took root. The volcanically formed mountains yielded an enormous bounty of gold and silver, and Durango developed quickly as a rail hub for shipping the rich ore to traders and smelters.

The rail remains important to the area's modern legacy as a link between past and present. The Durango and Silverton Narrow Gauge Railroad, rated among the ten best train rides in the world by the Society of American Travel Writers, demonstrates to passengers the importance of rail transportation in the rugged region's past, while offering a thrilling close-up of the gripping, mountain landscape.

Back in town, two designated National Historic Districts feature Wild West period buildings, and like the railway, stand as a testament to Durango's pioneer past. That spirit persists to this day as Durango has emerged as a business and cultural leader in the region, and the 14,000 townspeople have gained an international reputation for their friendliness to visitors.

But it is the Sheraton Tamarron's Cliffs golf courses, a Golf Digest Top 75 selection, that has put Durango on the map. The middle tee rating of 70.5 with a 135 slope gives clear indication that there is plenty of golf challenge to complement the stunning vistas. Old growth ponderosa pines and aspen trees dominate the course's 750 acres of cliff and canyons, and place an absolute premium on the tee shot finding the bluegrass fairways.

If not, scrub oak and underbrush can gobble errant golf balls the same way native whistle pigs occasionally do. Heed the local rule covering theft of golf balls by the yellow-bellied marmots, nicknamed whistle pigs for the shrill chirp they emit. These are small harmless mammals which burrow in the mountainsides, but occasionally amuse themselves – and passing foursomes – by darting across fairways to retrieve round white souvenirs for their mantle.

That hazard aside though, the real challenge of the Cliffs is to divert your attention from the scenery long enough to focus on Hill's myriad on-course obstacles. At the 395 yard, par four first hole, the character of the course is revealed immediately. With saw-toothed, granite cliffs rising in the north on Needles Mountain, the player must concentrate on an approach shot from 75 feet above a green completely engulfed by sand and water. There may be no more difficult club selection made on the day, as the decision must factor both the elevation drop and the 10 to 12 percent distance the altitude adds.

Then hope that by the time you've reached the seventh and eighth holes, you are correctly computing the carry of your irons, because these par fours present a pair of troublesome approaches over natural hazards. The second shot at the 415-yard seventh hole traverses a wide canyon, while a pond lurks at the green's left side. And the 355-yard eighth hole is no pushover with a stream dividing the fairway's right perimeter from a green setting across the hazard.

Since Troon Golf reversed the nines after taking over management duties, the current trio of finishing holes is a splendid culmination of the spirit of the course.

The 150-yard, par three 16th hole is a test of precision

Thunderstorm Over Tamarron
By Ray Wharton

to a long narrow green guarded by water at the front, right, and left. The 470-yard, par five 17th hole is a test of judgement whether or not to challenge a lake on the right, potentially setting up a second shot into the green, or play safely to the left, making it a three shot approach. And finally, the 380-yard 18th hole – perhaps Tamarron's best par four – is a test of nerve trying to avoid the landing area's right side water hazard, and then following with an approach to a long narrow elevated green bunkered on both sides.

Ultimately though, the reward of a Tamarron adventure is gleaned from one's appreciation for the unique combination of heritage and pioneering spirit that both emboldens the town and distinguishes the Cliffs course as a genuine masterwork of golf course architecture in the Colorado mountains.

Squaw Creek
SQUAW VALLEY, CA

"The more spectacular components, the better." That's what renowned artist Jim Fitzpatrick looks for when selecting a scene to paint, and Squaw Creek, located in the High Sierra of Nevada just five miles from Lake Tahoe, fulfills the requirements beautifully. "The Squaw Creek background is a crystal clear, blue mountain sky; a gigantic granite mountain; and a pine-covered slope. A reflective pond and the golden fall meadow grasses make up the foreground," reflected Jim. "These numerous ingredients so naturally complement one another, making the golf scene one of my favorites." It is no wonder that Squaw Creek ranks among many golfers' favorite courses as well.

Set in a fertile valley brimming with vibrant wild flowers, ponderosa pines that play home to deer and elk, and surrounded on three sides by mountains, the links-style course was designed by coveted architect Robert Trent Jones, Jr., in 1992. Jones and senior designer Kyle Philips went to great lengths to preserve the natural habitat and all of its resources. Using only 80 acres of playable land, they took care to maintain the native wetlands. "Basically it's a wetland with a golf course in it," said construction superintendent Carl Rygg. Tees, fairways, and greens are strategically placed to avoid disturbing the ecological balance of the forested hillsides which encircle them. Raised wooden cart paths were built to further minimize any threat to the environment. So perfectly in harmony with its surroundings, it appears to many that the course virtually disappears into the rugged Alpine backdrop.

The area was carved millions of years ago by glacial ice and is now famous for its crystal clean, thin mountain air, another valuable resource painstakingly protected by the developers. No pesticides are used anywhere in the resort complex, which resides at an elevation of 6,200 feet. Squaw Creek's commitment to the environment has earned them significant recognition, including being named "the most environmentally friendly course in North America," by several publications, and "perhaps the nation's most ecologically-sound golf course" by "Golf Course News." Audubon International immediately recognized Squaw Creek as a Certified Cooperative Sanctuary.

Jones himself said, "It is not often that a golf course designer has the opportunity to place a golf course in the midst of such spectacular surroundings. Our first and lasting vision was and still is that this course should blend in with the meadows, the slope, the trees, and the mountains. I think we have achieved this goal." Achieve it, they did, to the recognition of many. "Golf Digest" named Squaw Creek one of the Top Five New Best Courses and "Golf Magazine" ranked it among the Top Ten Courses You Can Play.

All 18 holes of the championship course wrap around a horseshoe-shaped meadow. Five holes play into rather steep mountain terrain, and, as can be expected, intimidating water hazards play a part in many. "It requires strategic play and greater accuracy," noted Rygg, "because target set areas are smaller and the penalties for missed shots are naturally greater."

Squaw Creek is known internationally as the home of the 1960 Winter Olympic Games, with great skiing still being a major draw for the resort. In addition to the tremendous golf facility, resort guests can also enjoy tennis, horseback riding, fly fishing, hiking, and mountain biking. "Conde Nast Magazine" has named Squaw Creek one of the Best Places To Stay In The World. Not much more needs to be said than that.

6th Hole
By Jim Fitzpatrick

5th Hole - Witch Hollow
By Jim Fitzpatrick

Pumpkin Ridge

CORNELIUS, OR

It didn't take long for renowned golf course architect Bob Cupp to realize he had been given a great parcel of land on which to build a course, or to realize that this site could support not just one, but two extraordinary golf courses. Cupp had been called to the Portland, Oregon, area of the Pacific Northwest to discuss the design and construction of a golf course that would fulfill the dream of three of the area's most avid golfers: Marvin French, Gay Davis and Barney Hyde. Determined to create the ultimate golf club, dedicated solely to the sport of golf and its enthusiasts, and capable of hosting a major championship, the team of French, Davis, and Hyde searched the area for a location worthy of their dream.

Finally, after over a year of dedicated searching, a 341-acre area just west of Portland, on the edge of the Willamette Valley, was secured. Cupp, who had worked with Jack Nicklaus for 14 years, was selected as the architect. Aside from his experience and reputation, it was his sincere enthusiasm about the project that most impressed the partners.

Fortunately for all who love golf, Cupp was able to convince the owners that the land was capable of supporting 36 championship caliber holes, and that the project could successfully be operated as a "mixed facility." The first course was planned as a private equity club, and the second as an equally challenging public layout. The entire complex was named Pumpkin Ridge Golf Club, with each course having its own name: Ghost Creek for the public course and Witch Hollow for the private course. Cupp took delight in challenging himself to design a public course that was so outstanding it would cause people to compare it equally or favorably to its private sister course. He did just that. People have been singing the praises of both, while arguing about which has stronger merits, since they opened in 1992.

The two courses are linked by a 320-yard, double-ended practice area that runs between the two clubhouses. While both are traditional in design, each course is singularly distinctive. Ghost Creek, the par 71 public course, can be stretched to 6,839 yards, resulting in a slope of 135 and a course rating of 73.6. While it is viewed as wide-open and on the short side of 7,000 yards, don't be lulled into complacency. Balls have a tendency to roll into lateral trouble on this course. The course opens and closes in an old meadow that has been reshaped into a pair of lakes, and a man-made stream that pops up and then disappears throughout the round is aptly referred to as Ghost Creek, hence the course's name. In addition to the water hazards, towering Douglas firs inject an entirely different challenge.

Witch Hollow, the 7,017 yard private course, takes advantage of the natural landscape of tall rye grasses and ancient towering oaks, which lent a level of maturity to the course even in its youngest days. Elevated greens and a variety of fiercely challenging bunkers contribute to the 141 slope and 74.8 rating the course has received.

Both Ghost Creek and Witch Hollow feature bentgrass

tees, fairways, and greens, and interestingly, Cupp designed both with five par threes and five par fives. He is particularly fond of creating holes that require a variety of shots, and all of the par threes have garnered widespread praise. Walking is permitted, and even encouraged, on both courses.

Fulfilling his commitment to the thrill of the partners, Cupp built a club that was capable of hosting a major championship. Within four years of its opening, Pumpkin Ridge hosted two Nike Tour Championships and landed two of the United States Golf Association's most important events: the US Amateur Championship in 1996 (best remembered for the thrilling sudden-death duel between Tiger Woods and Steve Scott) and the U. S. Women's Open in 1997. This was a remarkable accomplishment for a club so young in its development, but while it was unheard of, it disappointed no one. Pumpkin Ridge will continue to build on its growing reputation as a club worthy of attention and praise. It is especially refreshing to know that a public golf venue can elicit such strong opinions from those who feel it is superior to its highly regarded private sister course. The dream of three avid golf lovers and one extremely talented golf architect became a reality at Pumpkin Ridge.

St. Ives

STANWOOD, MI

Occasionally there is a parcel of land which captures the imagination and demands special attention. The natural wildlife preserve and wetlands located on the Canadian Lakes development, north of Grand Rapids, Michigan, is a true example of just such a find. When owners Norm Browning and Bob Doerr walked this property in the crisp, cool fall of 1992, they saw a magnificent collage of glacial carved hills and valleys, sparkling lakes, and deciduous woods that were home to deer and abundant wildlife. They wanted to create the very best recreational use for this spectacular and distinctive land in order to do it justice, which prompted the birth of St. Ives Golf Club.

Preservation of the natural surroundings was paramount when determining the layout of the course. Golf course architects Jerry Matthews and Lori Harmon worked in tandem with Browning and Doerr to sculpt a challenging and unique work of art that blended beautifully with the delicate landscape. Innovation was a key element in their design plans, as was evidenced by their introduction of the first suspended, elevated tee in the Midwest, supported by pilings as deep as 100 feet. They incorporated the wetlands creatively throughout the course, leaving some to pose as natural hazards. Numerous

1st Hole
By Paul Kuchno

elevated tees rise from the contours of the course in varying degrees, offering the golfer a multitude of breathtaking views and exquisite shots.

The tone of the course is set immediately on the first tee. As depicted in Paul Kuchno's watercolor, this picturesque hole boasts a beautiful view of Lake Mecosta, with oak, maple, birches, and pine trees offering vivid color contrasts, particularly throughout each change of season. The song of wildlife can be heard rising from the wetland alongside the ninth hole, which has unusual depth and a fascinating approach. The dramatic 14th hole, sprinkled with wildflowers, is unforgettable. In truth, almost any one of St. Ives' 18 holes could qualify as a signature hole.

Even the par threes are completely different and memorable. All are surrounded by water or wetlands, and

graceful aspens provide the backdrop for watercolor tees and greens. Watch for the nesting loons in the huckleberry marshes, and prepare to lose your concentration when a pair of bald eagles soar in for a landing at the fertile feeding grounds.

Significant attention went into fashioning the 26,000 square-foot clubhouse, known as St. Ives Manor.

Deliberately designed to look as though it has been there for decades, the Manor blends beautifully with the style of the course and surrounding landscape. Gracious and inviting, the country French clubhouse offers a comfortable setting in which to spend time and relax. It is immediately apparent by the overall positioning of the facilities that this building is dedicated to the golfer.

St. Ives has developed a strong following among golf enthusiasts and has received the recognition of the golf media as well. Rated by "Golf Digest" in 1997 as the Fifth Best Public Golf Course, St. Ives has earned a place among the most notable courses in America, and rightfully so. It has often been said that a day at St. Ives is the most soul-satisfying, beautiful day of golf in Michigan. We as golfers are grateful to the landowners for their original desire to create such a special golf venue and for their commitment to achieve such superb results.

St. Ives Manor
By Paul Kuchno

12th Hole
By Dave Chapple

Pelican Hill
Newport Coast, CA

How often does a golf course architect have the advantage of stepping onto a palette full of colors when designing a course? This opportunity is exactly what five-time Golf Course Architect of the Year, Tom Fazio, was given when he stepped onto the 451-acre parcel of land along the Pacific Coast Highway in Newport Beach, California, that is now home to Pelican Hill Golf Club. The azure ocean, sparkling like diamonds in the dazzling orange glow of sunshine; the rich, lush shades of grass, trees and vegetation spanning the green spectrum; the cerulean sky with barely a wisp of cloud; the rocky cliffs of sienna and bronze: these are only a few of the hues that belong to the natural landscape, and Fazio used them all to mold a masterpiece that will inspire awe in every golfer.

Pelican Hill Golf Club was one of the many projects masterminded by Donald Bren, a majority shareholder in The Irvine Company, which was responsible for the creation of Orange County and the Newport Coast. One of the company's primary missions was to design its projects with the goal of bringing people in closer harmony with nature. Pelican Hill is its internationally acclaimed focal point. "The Irvine Company was determined to make the Ocean South Course among the country's most spectacular," states Fazio. "Their commitment to quality, innovation and doing the job right has made that goal a reality."

After decades of planning and approvals, the much anticipated Ocean South Course opened in November, 1991, to outstanding reviews. "Golf Magazine" named Pelican Hill Golf Club one of the Top Ten New Resort Courses in 1991, and "Golf Digest" awarded it Best New Resort Course in 1992. Fazio's second masterpiece, the Ocean North Course, opened in 1993 to similar accolades, including its rating by "Golf Magazine" as one of the Top Ten New Resort Courses in 1993. Fashioned in the fine Scottish links tradition, this course meanders back and forth along an elevated plateau situated high above the deep-blue Pacific, with sailboats breezing along the ocean in the distance.

Obviously, Pelican Hill was an immediate success. Offering the ambience of a fine country club, yet open to the public, the course is a favorite among golfers, no matter what their level of skill or travel experience. The overall quality of the golfing experience at Pelican Hill is arguably among the best anywhere, with few rivals. The breathtaking panoramas are enhanced by the sounds of the surf against the rocks, while sea sprays catch soft, cool breezes. Squadrons of pelicans, the inspiration for the course's name, can often be seen out for their early morning feedings. Though they are beautiful, these birds pose an unusual natural hazard that golfers must often negotiate. Fortunately, they prefer fish to golf balls.

How often does the phrase "it simply doesn't get any better than this" really fit? One well-traveled golfer summed it up perfectly when he said he would gladly pay the full greens fees at Pelican Hill for the privilege and experience of playing just three holes. "'It simply doesn't get any better than this" fits at Pelican Hill. From the early Gold Rush days, dreamers have flocked to California in search of the proverbial pot of gold. For every golfer, Pelican Hill Golf Club is that pot of gold.

Fishing Fleet
By Dave Chapple

Cog Hill
CHICAGO, IL

Chicago has long possessed a large collection of world-class golf courses to accompany its rich tradition of hosting major professional and amateur golf championships. Unique among these golf facilities is Cog Hill, a collection of four courses, all accessible to the public, that is home to the PGA Tour's Motorola Western Open and was the site of the 1997 U.S. Amateur Championship. The story behind this collection of thoughtfully designed, well-maintained, and popular courses belongs to the patriarch of Chicagoland golf, Mr. Joe Jemsek.

For over half a century, this unpretentious bear of a man has devoted most of his waking hours to every aspect involved in the operation, maintenance, and promotion of quality, publicly accessible golf facilities. As a teenager, Joe caddied at Chicago area courses and began his professional golf career at age 17. Choosing to concentrate on golf course operation instead of playing professionally, Joe learned everything about golf operations in preparation for his career as owner. His first golf course, St. Andrews, was

18th Hole - Dubsdread
By Tom Lynch

13th Hole
By Libby Peper

acquired in 1939 and now consists of 36 holes. But it is Cog Hill which will be his primary golf legacy to the many Chicagoland faithful who fill his seven area courses from dawn till dusk during the season.

Dubsdread is the flagship course of Cog Hill's four-course complex. Designed by the highly regarded Dick Wilson and Joe Lee, it opened in 1964 and today is considered one of the best courses on the PGA Tour, a fact demonstrated by the strong fields this event consistently attracts. The three other courses at Cog Hill are all challenging, well-maintained layouts, over rolling terrain similar to Dubsdread.

In addition to Cog Hill and St. Andrews, Jemsek and his son Frank developed Pine Meadow Golf Club in the northwest Chicago suburb of Mundelein, a golf course favored by many seasoned golfers. Like its brethren, Pine

8th Hole
By Libby Peper

Meadow also features extensive practice facilities and quality golf instruction.

Jemsek's contributions to high quality, publicly accessible golf have brought him many accolades and honors. "Golf Magazine" named him one of its 100 Heroes of Golf, and the USGA selected him to its Executive Committee to contribute his leadership and vast experience.

If you visit a Jemsek course, do not be surprised to see a big, stately, mature gentleman in a blue blazer, white shirt, and tie, wearing a white bucket hat. Most likely, that will be Joe making sure his players are enjoying their round and the facilities he has been providing for more than 50 years to Chicagoland area golfers and visitors. And if you see him, tell him "Hello, Joe, and thanks."

18th Hole
By Libby Peper

Alcatraz, 17th Hole - Stadium Course
By A. J. Rudisill

PGA West
La Quinta, CA

Reflections, 9th Hole - Stadium Course
By Jim Fitzpatrick

Both Pete Dye and Jack Nicklaus have been described as "diabolical" at various times during their golf course design careers. Most often, that type of description is uttered by players who have simply bitten off more than they can chew on a championship (in the truest sense of the word) course designed by one of these two masters. In actuality, both architects only honor the wishes of those who commission their work, and they have no intention of inflicting pain and suffering on the unsuspecting golfer.

At PGA West Resort in La Quinta, California, both Dye and Nicklaus were directed to create a course that would be a Herculean test of golf located in a visually stunning desert setting. The sheer number of golfers who have tested their skills on these two masterpieces of classic desert target golf is a testament to the design success of both men. Tee it up at either of these desert monsters and get ready for a memorable round of golf. One might wonder how many average players actually keep score on either of these courses, or whether ultimately the goal is simply to be able to say, "I played it." More appropriate, perhaps, would be, "I survived it."

The numbers on both courses give a preview of what lies ahead. TPC Stadium Course, designed by Dye, plays to 7,261 yards from the back tees, and carries a slope of 151 and a course rating of 77.3. The Nicklaus Resort Course plays to 7,126 yards from the back tees, and carries a slope of 138 and a course rating of 75.5. The fact that a scratch player will be fighting to break 80 ought to tell you something about the challenge of these layouts. Both courses often require long carries over water or desert terrain on tee shots and approach shots to many of the large, undulating bent grass greens that are protected by unique sand bunkers.

If there is such a thing as a "typical" Pete Dye course,

TPC Stadium Course is it. Unlike many layouts where architects make a point of noting how little dirt was moved around to create the course, Dye unabashedly moved millions of cubic yards of earth. Starting with flat agricultural land, Dye made lakes, mounds, undulating fairways, and deep sand bunkers, then sprinkled target landing areas among them. While many of the greens are large, Dye strategically placed a number of smaller greens for challenge and variety.

All of the holes on both the Dye and Nicklaus courses have names, and among the most notable and memorable holes on the TPC Stadium Course are named Alcatraz, Amen, and Reflection. It is easy to see from Tony Rudisill's stunning artistic rendering just how Alcatraz earned its name. Tee shots are launched over water from an elevated tee box to an island green that is surrounded by water.

Amen is a 255-yard, par three that requires a long tee shot over water to a large green protected by still more water to the right (this is supposed to be the desert?). Even though there is a little margin for error allowed to the left, this hole cannot be taken lightly and was instantly rated one of the 18 toughest holes in America by the PGA when the course opened in 1986.

Reflection, the 450-yard, par four ninth hole, is a dogleg right requiring a long drive and an approach shot to a two-tiered green surrounded by sand bunkers. There is water (surprise, surprise) on the right that runs the entire length of the hole. "Golf Magazine" was so impressed with the hole that they placed it among their 100 Greatest Golf Holes in America.

The Nicklaus course also demands long, accurate tee and approach shots, with harsh penalties for errant shot direction. One of the unique holes here is the par four fifth, measuring 357 yards and aptly named Wishbone. The hole features a waste area running down the center of the fairway, affording players the choice of hitting their tee shot to either the left or right of the hazard. Players must factor in pin-placement and, to some degree, whether they should fade or hook the ball, when determining their choice of a landing area. The green is only 20 yards deep and is protected by sand in the front, back, and on the left side.

The 470-yard, par four ninth is the number one handicap hole on the course. The deep green is shared with the 18th, and approach shots must carry the last 110 yards over water to the hole. Play this hole carefully ... it is named Jack's Revenge. Maybe a little diabolical after all?

Either of these two great courses presents a challenge that is daunting to even the finest golfers in the world. In keeping with the rest of the resort, the impressive clubhouse and extensive practice facilities are world-class. Numerous competitions have been held at PGA West, including the Bob Hope Chrysler Classic, the Skins Game, the PGA Grand Slam of Golf, the Liberty Mutual Legends of Golf, and the PGA Tour Qualifying Tournament. Imagine having the fate of your professional golf tour career dependent on how well you handle the challenges presented by one of these two courses!

When you play PGA West, enjoy the beauty that surrounds you, from the perfectly manicured fairways and swaying palm trees, to the vibrant bougainvillea and the mountain backdrop. Appreciate the incredible talent of the course architects. Realize just how good the tour professionals are. Arrive with all aspects of your game tuned. And be happy just to survive.

Pasatiempo
SANTA CRUZ, CA

When thinking of the great golf courses of California, one is immediately drawn to the Monterey Peninsula, which contains Pebble Beach and Cypress Point, the masterpiece designed by the Scottish architect Dr. Alister MacKenzie. No golfing trip to this part of America, however, can be complete without experiencing Pasatiempo. Just one hour further up the coast from Monterey in Santa Cruz is what golfing aficionados call a "hidden jewel." Not only is the golf course a demanding challenge, it is also steeped in golf history. The vision and inspiration for Pasatiempo actually started at Cypress Point.

The historical connection is that Dr. MacKenzie designed both. Perhaps more important, but less known, is the input of Miss Marion Hollins, originally from Long Island, New York, and later a resident of California. She was one of the most accomplished sportswomen of her time. Recognized as a star equestrian, she was one of the best women polo players in the world. She was also a very accomplished lady golfer, as evidenced by her victory at the U.S. Women's Amateur Championship in 1921. She was later to become the first Captain of America's Curtis Cup Team.

Few remember her today for perhaps her greatest accomplishment, which was her involvement in the contruction of the Women's National Golf and Tennis Club (1924), Cypress Point (1927), and Pasatiempo (1929). In 1930, the great sportswriter Grantland Rice wrote about Miss Hollins, stating that she was the moving spirit and leading star on these three enterprises. She worked hand-in-hand with Dr. MacKenzie at Cypress Point, and he gave her full credit for the design of the world-famous 16th hole, stating, "she teed up a ball, drove it 219 yards across the roaring ocean, and said 'lets put the green there.'" While collaborating on Cypress Point, she had located and purchased a large parcel of land she felt would also be suitable for another exceptional golf course.

Using her charm and salesmanship, she persuaded Dr. MacKenzie to apply his golf design wizardry in partnership with her to create Pasatiempo. The course was officially opened September 8, 1929, with a mixed foursome of golfing champions made up of no less than Miss Hollins, Bobby Jones, Glenna Collett, and the great British Amateur Champion Cyril Tolley.

Both Hollins and Dr. MacKenzie approached Pasatiempo with specific design philosophies. Miss Hollins felt there should be alternate lines of play on every hole, not just the direct line to the green. This permits the shorter hitter or the cannier player to attempt a safer line of direction. She called her concept "strategic golf" design.

Dr. MacKenzie agreed with Miss Hollins, but his vision is also recognizable in the boldness of designing the greens

and bunkers and also in the way he encourages the player to do something better than he or she has ever done before, but at the same time providing a safe route to the hole for those of less ability or courage.

The first nine holes are in open rolling country. The first hole goes steeply down hill towards the ocean and encourages the golfer to feel confident that however the first shot is struck, whether solid or topped, the results are going to be rewarding. Do not fail to stop for a moment of reverence while on the sixth fairway. About halfway up the fairway on the left side is Dr. MacKenzie's home, where he resided during an extended sojourn in the United States.

The second nine holes are of a considerably different character because they lie in more wooded country. Here you will find canyons and numerous natural features that might thrill the adventurous golfer so much that he disregards them. While risk versus reward is always present, caution should be exercised on several holes as a missed shot will be punishing to one's score. Dr. MacKenzie regarded the 16th hole as the best two-shot hole he ever designed - and possibly in all of golf.

Designed in the classical tradition when match play was the game and amateur golf was at its peak, Pasatiempo has remained true to its beginnings. Its first champion was Bobby Jones. The course record, a 63, was established by Ken Venturi while he was a collegian. Other amateurs (before becoming accomplished professionals) who attempted to better the record, but with no success, included Fred Couples, Johnny Miller, Mark O'Meara, Tom Watson, and Tiger Woods. On the women's side, Glenna Collett set the standard, and subsequent champions included founder Marion Hollins, Joyce Wethered of England, and the great Babe Didrikson.

In 1986, the U.S. Women's Amateur was held at Pasatiempo, where the best amateur women players from all over the world elected to dedicate their respective rounds in memory of Miss Hollins.

Today Pasatiempo is consistently ranked among the top 100 courses in the country and one of the top 25 public access courses. The course still possesses those qualities that both enhance and confuse a player's efforts to be objective and strategic. Distances do not compute. Undulations are misread. There are awesome sights that interfere with a player's concentration. It encourages emotional turmoil while at the same time displaying a harmony with nature that causes golfers to argue that there are few places more breathtaking and challenging. This image so impressed Bobby Jones that he invited Alister MacKenzie to work with him on the design of Augusta National - the venue of The Masters.

Dr. Alister MacKenzie
By Jim Fitzpatrick

16th Hole
By Jim Fitzpatrick

"I stepped onto the tee of the 16th hole at Mauna Lani and knew

that one of my most inspirational paintings lay before me.

The contrasts of ancient lava flows, teal blue lagoons,

emerald fairways, and cobalt blue ocean had created one of

the greatest settings in golf. Truly an inspirational scene

to golfer and artist alike." *Artist Jim Fitzpartick*

Mauna Lani

Kohala Coast, HI

The native landscape of Hawaii is rich in both history and the unique elements from which it was formed, and the magnificent 3200-acre luxury resort of Mauna Lani is no exception. Kalahuipua'a, the ancient name for the lands of Mauna Lani, is known in Hawaiian history as a spiritual area, as well as for the numerous archaeological sites in and around the resort. King Kamehameha the Great maintained his royal fishponds here, and nearby roughly 3000 petroglyphs were carved over the centuries into stark, prehistoric lava. Discovering Mauna Lani's legacy can be one of the most fascinating Hawaiian experiences.

Another unforgettable experience is playing Mauna Lani Resort's two golf courses, the Francis H. I'i Brown North Course and South Course, named after the sportsman and socialite of royal Hawaiian lineage who acquired the land. The rugged terrain for both courses was laid by volcano, and features the dramatic contrast of severe jagged lava against lush emerald grass. The roaring waves of the blue Pacific Ocean add sounds to the striking visual surroundings. A setting amidst such an extraordinary landscape offers an exceptional experience for any golfer, and these courses offer a challenge for golfers of all levels of ability.

The South Course is built on the 16th century Kaniku lava flow. Legend has it that if the Volcano Goddess Pele favors you, balls hit into the lava will miraculously bounce back onto the fairway! A wide range of dramatic mountain and ocean views adds to the enjoyment of year-round golf on this island gem.

The North Course is built on a lava bed much older than the South Course, and it winds through rolling terrain and kiawe forests which often come into play. A 230-acre protected archaeological district lies on the northern boundary of the course, while herds of feral goats frequent the entire course, moving from green to green cropping the grass and providing a unique natural hazard.

Designed by the Honolulu-based golf course architectural firm of Nelson and Haworth, the courses have received Gold Medal awards for design from "Golf Magazine." Looking at their beauty, it is no surprise to learn that they are the host sites of the nationally televised Senior Skins Game golf tournament. Embedded in the spectacular elements of the natural landscape, the courses stand as testimony to what environmentally sensitive golf course architecture can achieve.

Within the resort is The Mauna Lani Bay Hotel and the breathtaking Bungalows. If ever there was a property that deserved the title "luxury resort," this is it. Located on 29 oceanfront acres on the Big Island's Kohala Coast, Mauna Lani Bay is an exquisite blend of sophisticated luxury and Hawaiian-style hospitality. The main structure faces the ocean and is an atrium-style design, with waterfalls, fish- and turtle-filled ponds, and an abundance of native trees and plants. Each of the five distinctive and luxurious Bungalows is dedicated to a flower of Hawaii – The Orchid, Plumeria, Bird of Paradise, Heliconia and Hibiscus – and each has developed its own private tradition. Accordingly, the decor of each Bungalow reflects the flower after which it was named. The magnificent 4,000-square foot living space is serviced by a butler and maid, and private consultations with the hotel chef can result in custom-designed menus.

Over the years, world famous celebrities, luminaries, and heads-of-state have come to call their favorite Bungalow "home." Kevin Costner (during the filming of "Waterworld"), Dustin Hoffman, Billy Crystal, Danny Devito, and Rod Stewart are some of the stars who have splashed in their private Bungalow pool. Many guests have even requested a copy of their Bungalow's architectural plans so they could recreate this dream home for their own.

While the glorious fairways and greens are the main attraction, Mauna Lani also boasts The Tennis Garden, named one of "Tennis Magazine"'s Top 50 Greatest U.S. Tennis Resorts every year since 1983. For the sport fisherman enthusiast, there are plenty of leaping marlins to reel in and whales to watch while experiencing the breathtaking splendor of the sparkling blue Pacific Ocean. All in all, Mauna Lani is a complete and completely grand resort.

Sailfish
By Dave Chapple

9th Hole - Hill Course
By Jim Fitzpatrick

La Paloma

TUCSON, AZ

The fact that "la paloma" means "the dove" in Spanish might cause one to assume that the golf experience at La Paloma Country Club would be somewhat tame, but one would be mistaken.

La Paloma Country Club is a 27-hole complex located in the high desert county of Tucson, Arizona. Take your pick of any combination of the three nines, named the Canyon, the Hill, and the Ridge, and get ready for 18 holes of exhilarating golf.

Jack Nicklaus designed all 27 holes at La Paloma, which opened to rave reviews in 1986 and was named one of America's Best Resort Courses by "Golf Digest." Like most desert courses, many of the holes require a tee shot that must carry over valleys and canyons to a landing area, followed by an approach shot over more desert terrain to greens surrounded by bunkers.

Be aware of the fact that any combination of the nines will add up to 7,000 yards of target golf from the back tees, with slope ratings in the 150's. It is advisable to check your ego at the door and to be realistic about your ability.

Players can tee it up from any of five tee options on each hole, making it possible for everyone to have a pleasurable golf experience.

Though difficult, the layouts are a fair test. While many of the par fours surpass 400 yards in length, a number of the par fives are reachable in two. Low handicappers would do well to bring a good long iron game since there are a number of par threes that are over 200 yards, most requiring a carry over native vegetation. Were we presenting a hole by hole description, here you might discover the absence of a very common hazard – water. There are no holes where water comes into play. This is the desert. However, do not breathe too easily yet. Nicklaus very effectively substituted natural hazards for the watery one.

The resort at La Paloma has all the amenities expected of a first-class facility with 487 rooms, award-winning meeting and convention space and six excellent restaurants. Superb practice facilities and an outstanding pro shop offer a stong complement to the courses. If golf is not your only athletic passion, there are tennis courts, swimming pools, and a health club with racquetball courts. Sightseeing is also a favorite activity in the Southwest, and the Tucson area features many interesting attractions, from the Tucson Museum of Art, the Reid Park Zoo, and the Kitt Peak National Observatory, to the legendary town of Tombstone located nearby.

Jack Nicklaus is well-known for his magical desert course designs, and La Paloma is a stunning example of them. The surrounding scenery of the Santa Catalina Mountains and the dazzling desert terrain is beautiful and picturesque, so along with your dose of "skill level" reality, make sure you bring your camera.

Doves
By Dave Chapple

Adriano Manocchia

8th Hole - Quarry
By Adriano Manocchia

Bay Harbor

BAY HARBOR, MI

Treasures abound in the lands of northwestern Michigan, proudly displayed for all to see. Rich forests, plentiful lakes, gentle hillsides, and golden meadows are visually fulfilling, with temperate lakeside breezes that grace the air and awaken the senses. Picture-perfect sunsets are vivid and alive with glowing hues of orange, much like the kaleidoscope of autumn colors radiating from the famous fall foliage of Michigan's hardwood forests on cool, crisp mornings. When spring arrives, the forest floor responds with a blanket of white trilliums and a tasty crop of morel mushrooms.

Blended with the marvels of these natural treasures exist some glorious man-made contributions: golf courses. The first courses, and arguably still the best, were created as part of the Boyne Highlands/Boyne Mountain legacy, a legacy that owes its heritage to the canvas of woods and waters on which it was born. The first of Boyne's courses was built in 1965 at Boyne Highlands. As interest in golf began to swell to its current epidemic proportions, Boyne grew right along with it, and the resort facility is now home to eight outstanding courses, spread from Harbor Springs to Petoskey, on the shores of Lake Michigan.

The exquisite jewel of the resort, Bay Harbor, is Boyne's most impressive project yet – and given its unusual foundation, perhaps his most interesting. Bay Harbor is set in what was formerly a quarry/cement plant. By the mid-1980s, it was in the grasp of industrial decay due to diminished supply of remaining limestone and obsolete equipment. Transformation of this depleted 1,100-acre gravel pit into one of the most desirable resorts in the country took ten years, an act of legislation, and millions of dollars. Historic Victorian architecture replaced massive thundering stone crushers; forests were replanted; and what was once a deep quarry pond is now a marina and yacht club; along two miles of Great Lakes shoreline, where gravel was once strip-mined, now stands the Bay Harbor Golf Club, three nine hole courses designed by world-class architect Arthur Hills. Prompted by the incredible changes from past to present, Bay Harbor was named Queen of the Debutantes at her debut.

Named Hills' crowning achievement, The Links, The Preserve and The Quarry pay homage to the diversity of the landscape by incorporating sandy beach dunes, quarry cliffs rising up to 200-feet above the water, thick stands of birch and cedar trees, and unsurpassed sweeping views of Little Traverse Bay. Bay Harbor did not have the advantage of a huge land mass on which to evolve, rather these courses were developed on a long, narrow site. As a result, its design is intimate and traditional, with tight fairways and small greens, requiring strong tee shots, delicate approaches, and pinpoint putting.

The Links is played primarily along Lake Michigan's Gold Coast, offering brilliant panoramic views of sparkling clear blue water, bringing golfers a welcome diversion after a misplaced drive or miscalculated putt. The sheer beauty of this setting provides much more than just a backdrop for great golf; if any course can be thought of as a perfect place to commune with Mother Nature, this is it.

Bordering the longest coastline of any course in the country, hundreds of acres of hardwoods play home to The Preserve. Dense forests of maples, beech, and poplars shade lush native flora, making an excursion into the rough an (almost) enjoyable experience. Often the only sound breaking the cathedral-like quiet of The Preserve is the melodic song of the birds perched in their natural habitat. Amid such tranquility and serenity, a loss of concentration is understandably commonplace, and completely forgivable.

Aptly named for its unique setting, The Quarry is built on rugged terrain that was once home to the former cement company's quarry. Five holes are built beside limestone cliffs, providing a dramatic setting and a stark variation from the soft padding generally associated with golf course landscapes. Strong and beautiful all at once, The Quarry is a study in contrasts and challenges. An elegant stone and stucco 12,000-square-foot clubhouse overlooks The Quarry's finishing green, giving a fitting finale to this most-talked-about course, touted as Hills' masterpiece.

Even before Bay Harbor joined the resort group's portfolio, Boyne Highlands and Boyne Mountain courses were held in high regard, and to this day they remain among the most coveted courses in Michigan. World-renowned designers Robert Trent Jones, William Newcomb, and Arthur Hills each created a masterpiece, ranging from The Heather with its wide tree-lined fairways; to The Moor, which confronts golfers with a water hazard at almost every hole and sports huge bunkers in front of roller coaster greens; to The Arthur Hills – scheduled for completion in 2000, a 7,037-yard course set among teeming bogs, oak groves, and pine-covered hills. The Donald Ross Memorial, ranked as one of Michigan's top six courses, recreated 18 of Ross' most famous holes from Inverness, Oakland Hills, Seminole, Royal Dornoch, and the famed Number Two at Pinehurst. The Monument Course begins atop Boyne Mountain and touts gorgeous vistas, while the Alpine Course distracts even intense golfers with dazzling views of nearby lakes and hills. And Crooked Tree Golf Club, inspired by the seaside courses of the British Isles and the Monterrey Peninsula afford dramatic high bluff views over Little Traverse Bay.

The facilities at Boyne Resorts offer golfers a tremendous variety of playing venues set in stunning surroundings. Because of an impressive list of architects and the exquisite landscapes on which they built, the golfing experience at Boyne USA is arguably among the best anywhere.

Troon North
SCOTTSDALE, AZ

All too often, the thought of Arizona desert golf invokes vivid images of standing on an elevated tee high above a vast expanse of sand, rocks, and cactus, searching far and wide for any oasis of green fairway in the distance. Thoughts turn to visions of navigating approach shots over enormous boulders, only to be faced with greens that are surrounded by even more sand. Perhaps this study in architectural and color contrasts would delight an artist, but would a golfer enjoy this venue? The answer is a definitive yes when the setting is Arizona's High Sonora Desert and Troon North Golf Club.

Located on the outskirts of Scottsdale, the complex is home to the Monument course, designed by the team of Tom Weiskopf and Jay Morrish, and Weiskopf's solo creation, the Scottish-style Pinnacle course. Troon North, named as a tribute to Weiskopf's 1973 British Open victory at Royal Troon in Scotland, is believed by many to be one of the finest golf facilities anywhere. While both courses take advantage of the natural landscape, they are uniquely different from one another, a design challenge Weiskopf accepted and accomplished in memorable fashion. The par

72 Monument course plays to 7,028 yards. Opened in 1990, it soon earned a national reputation as the standard by which other desert courses are judged. The inherent contours of the land were preserved along with many of the native natural hazards, including a 350 year-old cactus that was spared through creative design engineering on the fourth hole. Reassuringly, most of the hazards are in plain view, and the greens are large with subtle breaks. This is still target golf, though, and wayward shots should be avoided, as the wandering golfer is often rewarded if he is not careful with a dance among Gila monsters or a snag on jumping cholla. But the experience is well worthwhile, as the steep arroyos, natural washes, and forests of all varieties of cactus provide a stunning setting throughout the entire round.

"Bigger rocks and steeper drops" is a saying around Troon used in describing the huge boulders and striking elevation changes of the Pinnacle course. Here Weiskopf kept the rugged land in its natural state, which presented a myriad of design challenges. The 7,044-yard, par 72 masterpiece on such harsh landscape is a testament to his vision and ingenuity. With 82 bunkers, many of which are Scottish-style pot bunkers, it is fortunate that the greens at the Pinnacle are even larger than at its companion course. For the golfer who enjoys the challenge of getting to know

and appreciate the subtleties of a course, the Pinnacle is a must-play.

There are so many sensational holes on the course that Weiskopf had a tough time picking out a signature hole. Nonetheless, he calls the dramatic 299-yard uphill number six Canyon Pass hole "the best short par four I ever designed."

It is no wonder that both courses have received numerous accolades. The Monument course was ranked number 22 in America by "Golfweek Magazine," and is the only Arizona daily fee facility to be ranked by "Golf Digest" in its America's 100 Greatest listing. Troon North's two courses were ranked one and two in the state by "Golf Digest" in their ranking of Arizona's public access courses, and the editors gave the complex their five-star rating, one of only eight facilities in North America to receive the honor. In 1996, the Pinnacle course was nominated for Best New Course by "Golf Digest."

As many have found, the desert is a seductive place. For the golf enthusiast who enjoys developing an intimate knowledge and a true appreciation of the finer nuances of a course, Troon North may be the best the desert has to offer.

Desert Quail
By Dave Chapple

Torrey Pines
SAN DIEGO, CA

"I stood on the tee of the sixth hole and understood why it is ranked among the toughest 18 holes on the PGA tour.

Downhill, wind blowing in off the Pacific, bluffs on the left covered in coastal sage—you can't go long. What a magnificent setting for an artist to capture on canvas!"

Artist Dave Chapple

6th Hole - The North Course
By Dave Chapple

Just north of La Jolla, along a twisting, turning ten-mile stretch of California Coastline, you will find the Torrey Pines State Reserve, home of the rarest pine in the United States. Found only in this small region of San Diego County, the Torrey pine tree has long needles bunched at the ends of its branches that collect moisture from the coastal fog, which explains how it is able to survive the drought-like conditions in which it grows. These trees possess character, as do the two golf courses located among them, Torrey Pines North and South.

Torrey Pines is one of the premier municipal golf courses in the country, annually ranking in the "Golf Digest" Best Public Golf Courses edition. Located on the ocean bluffs just 20 minutes from downtown San Diego, the land was used during World War II for an Army training center, Camp Callan, and a gun emplacement area to protect the city from invasions. After the war, community effort brought about the construction of the 36-hole golf facility, which has been called "the ultimate Southern California golfing experience." It is now home to several annual PGA Tour events, including the Buick Invitational and the San Diego Open. The Junior Golf World Championships, which Craig Stadler and his son Keith won, making history as the first father-son team to win, are held here each July. Torrey Pines has also hosted the National Public Links Amateur Golf Championship, which fields the top 300 amateur players in the United States and provides the winner with an exemption to play in the U.S. Open and the Masters Tournament.

Both the North and the South Course feature several holes with stunning views of the Pacific Ocean to the west and mountains to the north. Deep canyons, thick with native wildlife and natural vegetation, provide both beauty, and a touch of fear at the thought of hitting into one. Although certainly inviting, the courses are not calm, and they are often deluged by fog, rain, and chilling ocean winds. It is never long, though, before that beautiful California sun shines brightly again.

The North Course is the shorter of the two, but considered by many to be more scenic than its sister. The signature par three, sixth hole is annually rated by PGA Tour players as one of the "18 Toughest Holes in Golf." There is a bluff on the left, covered with coastal sage and chapparal that makes a beautiful home for mother quail and her babies who seem to enjoy delighting the golfer. As seen in David Chapple's vivid painting of the hole, the natural beauty that surrounds you on the tee is a sight to behold. As your eye travels down the coastline toward La Jolla, and then downhill from the elevated tee, you realize that you simply can not go long, especially when the prevailing winds from the Pacific are at their strongest. As a matter of fact, it is considered a good rule to stay short of the greens, rather than shoot over them, on the entire course.

The South Course offers a superb challenge for both professionals and amateurs alike. Playing to 7,055 yards from the back tees, accuracy on long and mid-iron shots is vital to a good score. The 12th hole is considered one of the most difficult par fours on the PGA Tour. Whether it is the distraction of the hang-gliders hovering just beyond the green that gives the hole that distinction, or the fact that if you overshoot the green, your ball is flying off the cliff with the hang-gliders, is debatable. To reiterate, accuracy is vital on this course. Just ask Bruce Devlin, the inspiration for the name "Devlin's Billabong" given to the pond in front of the

18th. In the final round of the 1975 Andy Williams Open, Devlin took six shots to extricate his ball and ended up with a ten on the hole. Or ask Craig Stadler, who was disqualified from the 1987 Buick Invitational for violating the "building a stance' rule when he knelt on a towel and chopped his errant tee shot from the mud beneath a Leland cypress on the right edge of the 14th fairway.

Torrey Pines has earned many accolades including being ranked 16th in the list of best public courses in California by "Golf Digest," Torrey Pines was the only municipal course on the list. "Links" magazine put Torrey Pines South on its 50 Must-Play list. Fortunately, the courses are open year-round, allowing more than 95,000 rounds per year on each course.

One of the many jewels in the San Diego community, Torrey Pines is sure to make your must-play list, as well. One last tip ... the general lie of the land is towards the ocean, so most putts break in that direction. Accuracy.

California Quail
By Dave Chapple

15th Hole
By Adriano Manocchia

TPC Scottsdale
SCOTTSDALE, AZ

18th Hole
By Gordon Wheeler

Usually, the desert is thought of as a quiet, peaceful setting. At TPC Scottsdale, that thought was changed forever by one swing of the club. What golfer will ever forget when Tiger Woods' tee shot dropped into the cup on the par three, 16th hole at the 1997 Phoenix Open? The unprecedented sound of the roar from that day's crowd still echoes through the desert, immortalizing that shot as one of golf's all-time greatest moments and forever changing the feeling of desert golf at TPC Scottsdale. Now, for every golfer who steps on the 16th tee, the roar of the past crowd offers a surreal backdrop, and the thought that maybe, just maybe... well, you can imagine the rest.

TPC Scottsdale was built to accommodate both PGA Tour players and the general public. Managed by the PGA

Tour, it is one of only a few clubs in the network of Tournament Players Clubs (TPC) that is operated strictly as a daily fee, public facility. Set in the Sonora Desert with the McDowell Mountains rising above, and designed by the winning team of Tom Weiskopf and Jay Morrish, TPC Scottsdale offers two different golfing venues: the Stadium Course and the Desert Course. The course architects masterfully united challenge and playability to create two of the finest public courses in the country.

The TPC Stadium Course, designed expressly as the stage for the PGA Tour Phoenix Open, features trademark spectator mounding that promises an excellent view to everyone in the 400,000 plus galleries that gather for the Open. Because of its fan-friendly atmosphere, the Phoenix Open attracts the largest galleries of any tournament in the world. The tournament has become an event for every golf enthusiast or fan, combining the outstanding field of players with a lively atmosphere that is enhanced by ample refreshments and a multitude of excited spectators, thereby creating a memorable, fun experience for everyone.

Lush fairways are skirted by desert vegetation, and views of the surrounding mountains offer a spectacular setting for golf. One of the most dramatic holes on the course is the par five, 15th hole, beautifully captured on canvas by renowned artist, Adriano Manocchia. Only 501 yards, with water on the left side leading up to an island green, it dares the player to reach the green in two. The course is designed to provide a fair challenge (that is also forgiving) from the regular tees, while the back tees test even highly skilled players, making the course a favorite for golfers of all levels. The Stadium Course has received many accolades, among them a place in Top 10 Public Courses in Arizona and Top 25 Courses in Arizona by "Golf Digest." "Golf Week Magazine" called it "one of America's best courses" and "Golfer Magazine" named it among the Top 100 Golf Resorts in the World.

The Desert Course offers a more level landscape, with larger greens and fewer bunkers, but should not be taken for granted. Well-manicured natural terrain provides inherent hazards that are familiar to desert courses, and the prevailing winds present a different challenge each time the course is played. One of the most enjoyable holes is the sixth, a 193-yard par three, with a horseshoe shaped green surrounded by trees. An elevated tee on the eighth hole offers an incredible view of the valley, with the colors of the mountains creating a stunning backdrop. Voted by the Arizona Golf Association as Top 10 Best Value, and given the Eagle Award for Diamond in the Rough by The Best Golf in the West at affordable prices, the TPC Desert Course is an excellent facility at a reasonable rate.

Among the other awards honoring TPC Scottsdale, theirs has been named one of the Top 100 Golf Shops by Golf Shop Operations for ten consecutive years. The state-of-the-art practice facility is frequented by area-resident Tour professionals, who find it an excellent place to fine-tune the individual elements of their game.

TPC Scottsdale embodies the commitment to excellence that defines the 21 clubs in the TPC network. With the great surroundings, superior customer service, outstanding facilities, and that presiding ring of the roar of the crowd, there is nothing quite like desert golf at TPC Scottsdale.

9th Hole - Lakeside
By Tom Lynch

Cantigny
WHEATON, IL

The Gardens
By Tom Lynch

Colonel Robert R. McCormick is best remembered as the former publisher and editor of the "Chicago Tribune." Less well-known is his military service during WWI. As an artillery battalion commander in the U.S. Army's First Division, Col. McCormick was one of the military commanders in the Army's first offensive battle in Europe. The battle was fought and won in the French village of Cantigny.

Col. McCormick took the town's name for his 1,500-acre estate in suburban Chicago. The name now graces a remarkable golf course and grounds which include two museums, ten acres of gardens, and 27 holes of golf built on 500 acres of his former estate.

The ten acres of gardens include a wide and beautiful array of trees and plants. Golfers will see the influence of the gardens throughout their round as they are greeted at each hole by an abundance of varied trees, shrubs, and other plantings. Of particular interest are the topiary bushes that the golfer discovers during the round.

In this garden-like setting, noted architect Roger Packard skillfully conceived and executed 27 holes of golf, taking full advantage of the springs, ponds, and rolling terrain to give the golfer the sense of splendid isolation. Day lilies, poppies, chrysanthemums, and other colorful plants and shrubs combine with mature oaks, dogwood, birch, and linden trees to frame many of the holes. While not a heavily bunkered course, the ninth hole on the Lakeside nine features a large bunker in the distinctive profile of Dick Tracy, a long-time feature in the comics section of the "Chicago Tribune."

Golfers will also find extensive practice facilities, excellent golf instruction, a large clubhouse featuring a fine restaurant and lounge, a well-stocked golf shop, and ample meeting rooms.

After a relaxing round of golf on the beautiful course, Cantigny visitors can experience a part of history in the two museums, rich with the emotion of the past. The Robert R. McCormick Museum is housed in the former mansion. Indoor concerts are held in its library and outdoor concerts are conducted on the grounds every Sunday from May through September.

The First Division Museum and its research center contain historical papers and artifacts relating to the division as well as the archives of the "Chicago Tribune" and Col. McCormick's extensive collection of military history.

Thanks to Col. McCormick's vision and the energetic and dedicated stewardship of those who have followed, Cantigny will continue to provide a fine recreational venue for generations to come.

3rd Hole
By Libby Peper

Mauna Kea
KOHALA COAST, HI

Exciting. Breathtaking. Tough but spectacular. These are just a few of the descriptions that poured forth from renowned artist, golfer, and former NFL player David Chapple when he played Mauna Kea on the Kona coast of Hawaii. Perhaps most extraordinary to him and anyone else who has seen the course, is the incredible way in which the course is engineered into the striking terrain.

Prior to its opening in 1964, the land consisted of 150 acres of stark lava rock. The owner, Laurance Rockefeller, commissioned Robert Trent Jones, Sr., with the very difficult task of sculpting a course from this barren land. He correctly believed that the widely respected architect was one of a select few who could successfully tame the expanse. Jones had to pulverize tons of lava rock and coral to create the base for a unique strain of Bermuda grass that was used to seed the course. An innovative underground irrigation system contributed to the lush fairways and healthy greens that abound on the course. Maintaining the natural feel of the landscape, Jones left much of the native foliage, trees, and shrubs throughout, and created a design masterpiece that is remarkable in its ability to appear as one with the land. Mauna Kea has been ranked by both "Golf Digest" and "Golf Magazine" in their Top 100 Courses in the Country. "Golf Magazine" also honored the resort in its Top 12 Golf Resorts in America.

In the early 1980s, additional tees were added to create numerous options for the golfer. Perhaps the best example of the variety of possible tee shots is the celebrated par three, third hole, which offers six different locations from which to "tee it up." With a 200-yard carry over the dazzling blue waters of the Pacific Ocean, this is one of the most scenic and copied par threes anywhere, and has been named one of the Top 100 Holes in the World by "Golf Magazine."

The resort itself has received numerous accolades and offers a total experience for individuals and families alike. The tennis facilities are ranked among the best in the world, and those who desire the lure of deep sea fishing will revel in the quantities of sailfish and marlin that abound. Nature lovers will delight in watching huge manta rays swim right into the lagoon, while the song of vibrant tropical birds reverberates all around. Be sure to watch out for the Hawaiian cardinal, a striking red, gray, and white bird that is substantially bolder than its mainland U. S. counterpart.

Mauna Kea features rolling fairways with dramatic elevation changes and views of the sparkling blue Pacific and Mauna Kea Mountain. Even Mother Nature offers her special touch - gentle ocean breezes that help make a round at Mauna Kea unforgettable.

3rd Hole
By Dave Chapple

Diablo Grande
PATTERSON, CA

In the historic ranchlands of western Stanislaus County in central California, there is a valley populated with impressive stands of blue and valley oaks, running creeks and plunging canyons, vineyards bursting with sweet fruit, and sun-splashed hillsides where native wildlife roams free. It is here that you will find Diablo Grande, the brainchild of legendary entrepreneur Donald Panoz.

Along with an talented partnership of experts in the fields of resort planning, land use, golf course architecture, and water resources, Panoz designed a 33,000-acre master-planned community, 12,000 acres of which have been set aside for permanent wildlife preservation. When completed, the community will feature six championship golf courses, world-class recreational amenities, an elegant resort hotel and spa, an executive conference center, diverse residential neighborhoods, and nearly 45 acres of vineyards, reminiscent of Panoz's original golf resort and winery masterpiece in Atlanta, Chateau Elan.

Above all, Diablo Grande is serious about its golf. Here, golf is a remembrance of things past, of a time when tradition, gracious hospitality, charm, and elegance were a

12th Hole - Ranch Course
By Matt Scharlé

Scharlé '97

way of life – a time that we recall fondly remembering the era when golf's legends ruled the game. Diablo Grande prides itself on its return to the traditions of the game's illustrious past, from the old-world service that greets you upon arrival to the way the beautifully maintained championship courses reside in harmony with nature, complementing the native terrain, rather than imposing themselves on the landscape.

Two tournament-quality courses currently exist at Diablo Grande: the Ranch Course and, quite appropriately, the Legends West Course, named not only for the legends of the game it represents, but also for its sister course in Georgia, named simply The Legends at Chateau Elan.

The Ranch Course, designed by award-winning architect Denis Griffiths, sprawls across 178 acres of stunning surroundings, winding through oak trees, across creeks, and through vineyards. Playing to 7,200 yards, the Ranch Course is long and narrow, with a challenging array of bunkers and water hazards, placing both distance and accuracy at a premium. Mother Nature's influence surrounds you with crisp fresh air, the hum of water tinkling over rocky creek beds, and the serene pastoral setting that awaits you at every turn. Combine all this with the thrill of competition, and you have a golf experience you won't soon forget. This is the way golf was meant to be played.

At the Legends West Course, you will immediately feel the influence of two Grand Masters of the game – Gene Sarazen and Jack Nicklaus. Panoz invited these two incomparables to design an awe-inspiring course, challenging yet rewarding, that would reflect their own signature styles. In grand fashion, they created a course that is unlike any other in the world ... a course that will take your breath away. The beauty is spread over 170 acres of spectacular land, playing to 7,100 yards. Generous contoured fairways are forgiving, but the small fast greens require a soft touch and an active imagination. The abundant bunkers are deep and can be quite punishing. The Legends West Course is considered one of the finest in northern California, and for good reason.

From the moment you arrive until the moment you sink your last putt, the goal at Diablo Grande is to make your visit a memorable one. Whatever it is about the experience of golf that moves you, Diablo Grande has it. From the breathtaking landscape to the unhurried pace of play on the tournament-quality courses, all enhanced by the superb club-like atmosphere and service, Diablo Grande takes golf to soaring heights.

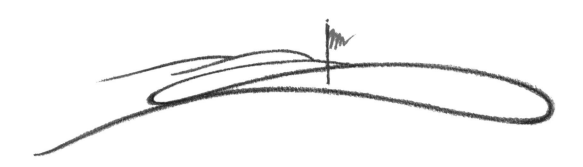

THE LEGACY OF AMERICAN GOLF

Featuring Portraits Of The Legends That Have Kept The Legacy Alive

By Sidney Matthew

In all of golf's 600-year history, there is perhaps no more remarkable story than the legacy of American golf. Most believe the Scots invented the game in the 1300s or before (the Dutch school claiming the origin of golf notwithstanding), and ever since, its popularity has captured the imagination of all industrialized civilizations. Because golf has challenged man's ingenuity to such an extent, it has become the greatest game ever conceived.

It is difficult but essential to acknowledge that the first fossils of golf history perhaps rest in a 14th century stained glass window of a golfer in Glouchester Cathedral in England. And that the first crucible of competition still reposes in the virtually unmolested sanctuary known as the Old Course of St. Andrews. Since 1208, three finger bones, an arm bone, and a kneecap of the namesake Apostle were directed in a vision experienced by St. Regulus to be taken to the western boundaries of the known world and established there as a suitable memorial. These remnants began the journey in Constantinople and made it as far as that rippling green peninsula jutting into the Eden Estuary on the east coast of Fife, Scotland.

From those primitive origins sprang forth a unique method to measure skill and chivalry among men totally apart from war and its grisly trappings. It constituted, as adroitly noted by Sir Winston Churchill, "a curious sport whose object was to place a very small ball into a very small hole with implements singularly ill suited for the purpose."

Many took up the challenge. Others occupied their obsession with making the clubs and balls and courses, and clothes and the necessary whiskey, which was the reward for all who labor in the first instance. The distillation of their affections yielded feather balls, thorn-headed play clubs, and courses with obstacles named Purgatory, Perdition, Hell, and the Devils Asshole.

The early founders of the game had every justification to be proud of what they had wrought. It was a splendid proving ground for athleticism and courage and character. Unlike fencing and archery, "gowf" permitted a sportsman to explore the boundaries of his innermost being in competition with himself and the obstacles of nature on the course. Somehow, a golfer realized the immediate emotional relief achieved by "killing" an inanimate object, the ball, as compared with killing a living enemy who would not be spared the luxury of returning to fight another day.

To the delight of today's 26.5 million golfers, the game was exported to America by brave and hardy souls long before the Constitution was debated and signed. The players, clubmakers, architects, and organizers didn't just carry their wives and children in the boats that landed in the Colonies. The ship's cargo manifests also included golf clubs and feather balls. With these implements and their knowledge and enthusiasm, the pioneers were able to establish golfing footholds in Savannah, Charleston, and Yonkers, New York. They built courses that featured strategic obstacles and options rather than the popular penal designs back home. And they laid the important cornerstones of American golf history, which even today are yielding rich dividends.

Long before the achievements of Hogan, Palmer, Nicklaus, Trevino, and Watson in the affairs of world championships, other men and women made lasting contributions enjoyed by all who came later. Some broke the ice by winning America's inaugural titles. Two others, Bobby Jones and Babe Zaharias, helped set the standards by which the greatest players in the world would continue to be judged even today. The legacy is quite remarkable.

Bobby Jones
By J.A.A. Berrie

In these early days, golf was simply a fledgling sport not taken seriously enough to be reported sooner than page two of the newspaper sports section. In Scotland the game's traditions were practiced by the common man on public courses, but in America the privileged classes took up the game first. Even so, by 1914 only 300,000 sportsmen identified themselves as "golfers." Their British cousins were not so sure. Actually, up to World War I, the British were not at all impressed by what they saw of American golfers. The U.S. Open was inaugurated in 1895, but it was not captured by a homebred American, Johnny McDermott, until 1911.

The manner in which the amateur champion golfer of the United States was first determined did little to impress the British either. The first contest at Newport, Rhode Island, Golf Club in 1894 was apparently won by W.G. Lawrence who returned the lowest two-day medal score of 188. This outcome was bitterly contested by the runner-up from Chicago, Charles Blair MacDonald. MacDonald was not

blessed with the virtues of immodesty and grace in defeat. He immediately whined and complained that the contest was unfairly conducted at medal versus match play and that the course was grossly unfair because it had stone walls meandering through the fairways. MacDonald further criticized a rules decision which assessed a two-stroke penalty against him when he improved his lie away from the stone fence. "We need to declare this a 'no contest' and hold another proper championship," he demanded.

Rather than establish a game of rules and not men, MacDonald's colleagues meekly bowed to his blustery challenge. A second championship was held the next month in Yonkers, New York. It was conducted at match play and hosted by the oldest continuously existing American club founded in 1888 by John Reid and the "Apple Tree Gang" named the St. Andrews Golf Club. MacDonald played well in his early matches, reaching the final match for the championship against L.B. Stoddart. MacDonald prepared

Francis Ouimet
By Walt Spitzmiller

for the match by partying until five a.m. Suffering from a severe case of "cocktail flu" the next morning, MacDonald decided to treat his illness with a steak and champagne lunch. With this accompanied by strychnine tablets, he played a respectable game, ultimately losing to Stoddart by only one hole. Again, however, MacDonald refused to acknowledge his defeat and to recognize the new champion. "I was sick," he said. And besides, a single golf club cannot itself confer a national title like the U.S. Amateur Champion on anyone. That should only be done collectively by all the golf clubs in the country. Thus was born the United States Golf Association in December 1894. It is somewhat anticlimactic that the third time proved to be the charm when C.B. MacDonald finally won the "inaugural" (and by MacDonald's thinking, first official) U.S. Amateur Championship in 1895 at the Newport Golf Club.

That same year Mrs. Charles S. Brown won the first U.S. Women's Amateur Championship at the Meadow Brook Club in Hempstead, New York. The event was a one-day medal play competition.

The next year the Ladies held their second U.S. Amateur Championship in October 1896 at the Morris County Golf Club in New Jersey. This year the event was a match play competition. The winner was Miss Beatrix Hoyt, who went on to win again in 1897 and 1898.

If American golf was to earn respect among the nations, men and women of extraordinary skill and character were desperately needed to come forward and forge the way. MacDonald's early example of integrity left something to be desired.

An important early effort to establish American respectability was made by an Australian-born transplant to America named Walter J. Travis. Travis took up the game at age 35 and was for that reason called "the old man" by his fellow competitors. Travis did not have the outward appearance of the quintessential golf champion. He was small in stature and not known for driving the ball a long way. What he lacked in distance, however, was compensated for by his deadly accuracy on both the fairways and greens. "The man who can putt is a match for anyone," Travis often said in remembrance of Willie Park's favorite line. Most importantly Travis practiced the best traditions of sportsmanship. He followed the rules to the letter and expected his opponents to do likewise. Sporting a black beard that spoke volumes about his reserved demeanor, Travis did not suffer fools easily on the golf course. He was respectful and polite to his adversaries, but his emotions were buried deep from the surface. One observer of Travis wryly quipped, "If you stuck an ice pick in him, I bet he'd bleed ice water." There was no doubting the old man's ability to bring home the silver. In 1900, he won his first and in 1901 his second U.S. Amateur Championship, followed by a third in 1903. Maybe the old man who chewed on long black cigars could wrest a measure of respect for American golf by winning the British Amateur Championship. At least Travis thought he could do so in 1904 when he entered the field at Sandwich. But upon his arrival at St. Georges Golf Course, he was not joined in his ambition by his British hosts. They were not particularly enthralled by the "wee ice mon's" straight and direct style. "Surely, this audacious little American does not presume to have what is needed to expatriate our championship trophy," they seemed to communicate to Travis.

The British hosts initially extended the hand of friendship by inviting him to dinner. "Sorry," Travis told them. "I've got plans." "How about joining us for a drink after dinner," the hosts offered. "Sorry," Travis declined, "I'll just keep to myself and my friends." This failure to establish society did little to further diplomacy between the hosts and Travis.

Not only did the red carpet fail to roll out for the American, but he also got what he perceived as being tantamount to a royal snub. Whether he asked for it or not with his brazen demeanor, Travis

Gene Sarazen
By Linda Hartough

Gene Sarazen
By Linda Hartough

got all he could handle and more. Could he stay in the guest quarters of the golf club? "Sorry," he was told, they were quite full. Could he have a locker in the club to change clothes and shoes? "Sorry," those are reserved for members. "You'll have to change in the hallway." Could he get a practice round with some of the better players in the field? "Sorry," they already have a game with their pals. Could he keep his clubs in the clubhouse? "Sorry," you'll have to use the professional shop. As if this was insufficient to raise Travis' dander, the "coup de grâce" was the caddy assigned to Walter for the championship. Sadly, the best attribute of the caddy was his crossed-eyes. He had no clue about the rules of the game, made numerous mistakes in each round, and repeatedly flagged the hole inappropriately for his player and opponents alike. Travis asked the boy where his drives went. "I don't know," was the usual reply. "I didn't see it." Travis went to the caddymaster immediately and tried to get a replacement. "He's a nitwit and an abomination," Travis complained. "Sorry," replied the caddymaster, "Not possible." Despite all this Travis' anger did not boil over. He pursed his lips and philosophically told his friends, "A reasonable number of fleas is good for a dog. It keeps him from forgetting he's a dog."

It is little wonder that Travis' game fell apart in the days preceding the championship. His putting was always the best part of his game, but that too totally deserted him. Desperate to try anything, Travis borrowed a centre-shafted Schenectady putter from his friend Edward Phillips on the day before play began. It worked like a charm. After winning his first match in a pouring rainstorm, Travis asked officials if he could change into dry clothes before his afternoon match. "Sorry," they told him. "There's no time unless you wish to default." Travis redoubled his resolve to win, toweled himself off, and mowed down his next opponent with his remarkable putting. He was soon the talk of the tournament. "I say, have you seen that American who is putting with that extraordinary thing like a croquet mallet?" whispered the patrons to each other. One by one, Travis' "enemies" fell. If they were not "enemies" before the matches, Travis did what he could to convert them against him during the campaign. He called a penalty on one player for soling his club in a bunker. And he made no idle chitchat with anyone before, during, or after his play. It was not unexpected that when the winning putt went down, none of the stunned gallery applauded.

The collective shock and disappointment of the people was evident in Lord Northbourne's presentation speech: "Never since the days of Caesar has the British nation been subjected to such humiliation .... It is my fervent hope that history might not repeat itself."

As if these remarks were not humiliating enough, the displeasure with Travis' centre-shafted putter was further punctuated when it was banned from future competition by R&A while the USGA kept it legal. This marked the first time that the USGA diverged from an R&A ruling.

Looking back on the event years later, Travis wrote: "It is doubtful if Lord Northbourne ever heard the story of the little girl who, leading a mongrel cur, was met by a man who said, 'What kind of a dog is that?' 'He's a mutt,' she said softly. 'But why do you whisper?' 'Sh-h-h, I don't want to hurt his feelings. He thinks he's a Japanese poodle.'"

It was not until 48 years later in 1952 that the ban on Travis' putter was lifted, and with more respect it was acknowledged that just possibly the man had posessed talent.

The message brought home with Travis was loud and clear. American golfers may not have the "pedigree" to win major championships, but they can persevere and win all the same with pride and pugnacity.

A 20 year-old mild-mannered former caddy from Boston, Massachusetts, got the message. Francis Ouimet won his state amateur championship and had qualified for the National Amateur, reaching the semi-finals. USGA President Robert Watson talked him into entering the 1913 U.S. Open Championship contested at Brookline. But nobody convinced Francis that he could not or should not win. After all, the "paladins of golf," Harry Vardon and Ted Ray, were across the pond for the championship and they were certain to win. Vardon and Ray had won nine major championships between them, including the British and American Opens. Each knew how to win and also how these things can be lost. Francis, on the other hand, played his own game and his mind was totally uncluttered with such details. His nerves were as tranquil as a baby's such that he actually gave a golf tip to an inquiring spectator during the final round! Even his ten year-old caddy, Eddie Lowry, had the poise to properly counsel Ouimet to "keep your eye on the ball" and "take your time, you've got all day." Not only did Francis tie Vardon and Ray at the end of 72 holes, he calmly beat them in the play-off.

Once Vardon was accosted by a lady in the temperance movement who preached to him the virtues of abstinence. "Madam," Vardon replied, "I agree moderation is good in all endeavors, but never have I failed to defeat a teetotaler."

When Francis Ouimet celebrated his Open victory at the Country Club the next day, he tossed down, one after another, a drink called Horse's Neck comprised simply of lemon juice and ginger ale. Ouimet proved that one need not be a "plutocratic snob" from a well-known country club to play championship golf. Nor was the game a private preserve of the professional ranks. In 1914, Ouimet won the U.S. Amateur Championship by beating previous four-time

Walter Hagen
By Bernie Fuchs

Harvey Penick
By Paul Milosevich

winner Jerome Travers in the finals. This feat gave Quimet another distinction. He was the first amateur to win the U.S. Open and the U.S. Amateur. In 1915, Travers became the second Amateur Champion to also win the U.S. Open.

Ouimet also proved another point when he won the U.S. Amateur in 1931. Herbert Warren Wind asked him why it took so long for him to collect another major. Ouimet delighted in his reply. "Did you ever hear of a boy from Atlanta named Bobby Jones?"

The last bastion of British golfing superiority to fall to Americans was the British Open. (They like to call it "The Open.") In 1921, a contingent of Americans led by Jock Hutchison and accompanied by 19 year-old Bobby Jones traveled to St. Andrews. The prior year, Jock had won the PGA Championship and had won three tournaments in 1921 before sailing to Britain. Considered the finest exponent of the mashie-niblic pitch, Hutch used a ribbed-faced club that imparted severe backspin to keep the ball on hard, slick, unwatered greens. In the first round, young Jones was treated to a rare feat. On the short eighth, Jock scored a hole in one. Then on the ninth, as Tom Kerrigan was replacing the flagstick into the cup, Jock's drive lipped out of the hole and finished only inches from his second ace in succession! Spectators erroneously reported that Kerrigan had seen the ball going into the hole and had run onto the green to pull the flagstick. At the end of play, Jock tied with amateur Roger Wethered. That evening, Jones and several other amateurs had to persuade Wethered to stay and finish the play-off. Wethered wanted to default because he had committed to play in a previously scheduled cricket match! No matter. Jock

prevailed in the play-off and became the first person to take the Open Championship trophy to America. And just for consistency, the ribbed-faced mashie used by Jock to produce the "stop-em" shot soon suffered the same fate as Travis' centre-shafted Schenectady putter. It, too, was banned from future competition.

Added to these historic occasions on which Americans first captured the world's major contests, there were other early high water marks in the legacy of American golf. Chicagoan Chick Evans collected the first "Double" in the same year by winning both the U.S. Open and the U.S. Amateur Championships in 1916. Having won the U.S. Amateur in 1922, Jess Sweetser became the first native-born American (Travis was born in Australia) to win the British Amateur in 1926. Gene Sarazen captured another "Double" in 1932 when he joined together the U.S. and British Open titles. And between 1921 and 1933, a span of 13 years, Americans won the British Open Championship a remarkable total of 12 times.

During this astonishing run, Walter Hagen made a special contribution. He won the U.S. Open in 1914 and 1919, while adding four British Open titles. "Sir Walter" also set a record of 22 consecutive PGA matchplay victories on his way to five PGA Championship titles. He collected 11 professional majors, which is second only to Jack Nicklaus. But Hagen did much more for the legacy of American golf than this. He elevated the status of professionals as persons worthy of the highest respect and admiration. Hagen was personally offended that golf professionals were treated as lower class citizens. Many early golf professionals were former caddies who had polished their skills. A good number didn't dress well, didn't speak well, and didn't behave well either. Servants of the wealthy establishment clubs were not permitted to enter through the front door. Nor were professionals treated any differently than servants. Hagen resolved to change the attitudes of the game's establishment single-handedly.

He ordered the finest clothes from Saville Row and New York's Fifth Avenue. On the golf course, Hagen dressed more elegantly than the club members. "I don't want to be a millionaire," he quipped, "I just want to live like one." Hagen was the first man to make a million dollars in golf, but he spent two. Hagen learned that the clubhouse at Deal, England, was off-limits to professionals during the British Open in 1920. No problem, he figured. He rented a Rolls Royce and parked it in view of the large windows from which the members peered. His chauffeur got out of the car, set up

Ben Hogan
By Walt Spitzmiller

a table with linen cloth and folding chair. Next, a champagne bucket was brought out together with a sumptuous lunch. The chauffeur then opened Walter's door, escorted him to the table, and served Walter to the astonishment of the club members. Hagen opted to change his shoes each day in the Rolls rather than avail himself of the professionals' tent. Hagen traveled with four trunks of clothes and an entourage that included a press agent and other hangers-on. He flew his friends on a rented plane to a nearby gourmet restaurant because the food suited his discriminating taste. Walter flirted with all the available ladies. "Call every woman 'sugar,' and you can't go wrong," he often advised the younger players.

Hagen did have some help in his quest to elevate the status of golf professionals. In 1928, both Hagen and Sarazen were invited by the Prince of Wales to play a practice round at the Royal St. Georges Golf Club. After completing nine holes, the Prince turned to his guests and inquired, "Would you gentlemen like to go into the clubhouse and have a libation before proceeding with the game?" Sarazen looked at Hagen and both of them smiled saying, "Of course, we would love to do that." The two professional golfers could hardly contain their glee as neither one of them had ever seen

the inside of the clubhouse. When they were seated, the headwaiter came over to the their table, bent down, and whispered into the Prince's ear. The Prince then gently pushed the waiter back so that everyone in the room could hear what he had to say. "Now see here, we'll have none of that. These two gentlemen are my guests and you will serve them or I'll take the Royal out of the Royal St. Georges." Both Hagen and Sarazen smiled broadly as they tipped their glasses with a small "tink" with that of the Prince. It was a small gesture but also a large crack in the armor of social convention regarding the acceptance of golf professionals.

Hagen was never a great ball striker but was able to pull off the trouble shot when it counted most. He never put too much pressure on himself, reasoning that nobody could play perfect golf. During a round, you were always going to miss a few strokes, so don't worry too much about it. One commentator quipped, "Hagen makes more bad shots in one round than Harry Vardon did in his entire career." Walter's opponents were often unnerved by his lackadaisical attitude on the course.

Hagen himself admitted the benefits of gamesmanship against his adversaries: "I always used a lot of strategy and *psychology and it often paid off. I used it on all of them. I set up shots the way a movie director sets up scenes...to pull all the suspense possible from every move. I strutted and smiled. I hooked and I sliced into the rough off the fairways, but how I clobbered that little white ball. When the chips were down, the gallery tense and my opponent either overconfident or sick with apprehension. Sure I grandstanded. But don't get the idea I was merely being amusing and brassy. To me that stuff was all part of my game. It helped fluster my opponent as much as it delighted the gallery...and was equally important in releasing the tension from my game."*

Hagen's charm and confidence won over the most hardened critics. The owner of the "The London Times," Lord Northcliffe, sent one of his reporters to interview Sir Walter. He was supposed to do a number on him and expose him for the phony that he surely was. After all, what kind of egotist would drive golf balls from the roof of the Savoy Hotel into the Thames River? Walter received the reporter at his suite in the Ritz Hotel wearing a purple silk smoking jacket. The reporter came away greatly impressed. Hagen was certainly no fool. He knew exactly what he was doing and why he was doing it. And he adroitly pleaded the cause of the golf professional and his rightful status in society. "We deserve your respect," Walter argued forcefully. The reporter returned and told his boss Northcliffe that Hagen was genuine and any story about him would have to be complimentary.

By making a similar pitch to other media, Hagen almost single-handedly turned the tide of public opinion to elevate the status of golf professionals. Gene Sarazen got it right when he declared, "All the professionals who have a chance to go after the big money today should say a silent thanks to Walter each time they stretch a check between their fingers. It was Walter who made professional golf what it is."

Of all the contributions to the early legacy of American golf, surely the cornerstone in the foundation was set by Robert Tyre (Bobby) Jones, Jr., of Atlanta. Even according to British appraisals, Jones' example represents the very best that can be said for American golf traditions.

It is arguable that the record he compiled in a relatively short 14-year career was extraordinary enough to set Jones apart from all who preceded and followed him. But that is not likely the compelling reason for Jones to be vaulted onto a pedestal of hero worship both at home and abroad. It was rather the manner in which Jones faced both Triumph and Disaster and treated those two imposters with equal measures of grace, courage, and dignity. In appraising the secret of Jones' unique gifts, the poet laureate of golf, Herbert Warren Wind, penetrated the truth when he observed: "He had incredible strength of character. As a young man, he was able to stand up to just about the best that life can offer, which is not easy. And later he stood up with equal grace to just about the worst that life can offer. On top of everything else, he had tremendous personal magnetism .... Jones, in short, was the model American athlete come to life, and it is to the credit of the American people that they recognized this almost instantly."

Jones single-handedly redefined the frontiers of golf history. Many of his records, including the "crown jewel," the Grand Slam, will never likely be eclipsed. But Jones achieved much more than recognition as the most distinguished athlete in his sport. By earning the respect of the world, he took on an unofficial ambassadorship for America that was

Sam Snead
By Bernie Fuchs

and still is unprecedented. When aviator Charles Lindbergh made his solo flight across the Atlantic Ocean, he received the adulation of two continents and was given a ticker tape parade down Broadway in New York. When Admiral Byrd first landed on the North Pole, he too was given a ticker tape parade. So was John Glenn when he became the first man to orbit the earth in 1962. Ben Hogan received the honor for his "Triple Crown" victories in 1953, winning all the major championships except the PGA.

Bob Jones is the only man in history to enjoy two of these ticker tape parades. The first commemorated his "Double" in 1926 when he captured both the U.S. and British Open Championships. He was honored again in 1930 during the year of his immortal "Grand Slam." Alistair Cooke has carefully observed American current events in his 50 years of broadcasting the weekly BBC "Letter from America." According to historian Cooke, Jones is the only man who was ever able to challenge Lindbergh's position as the quintessential American hero. Jones' popularity was perhaps more appreciated abroad than in his home country. He was conferred citizenship in 1958 by the Royal Burgh of St. Andrews. Only one other American has been so honored, almost 200 years earlier in 1759, Benjamin Franklin. Other great golfers have been bestowed with high honors by the Town and University of St. Andrews, the Home of Golf. Jack Nicklaus and Gary Player have received honorary degrees. Gene Sarazen, Peter Thompson, and others have been given the "Freedom of the Links," permitting them to play the Old Course at their leisure. Jones is the only golfer who has ever been invested with citizenship of the entire Royal Burgh. Jones' name adorns the same Book of Royal Burgesses that contains the names of the King, British Prime Minister Stanley Baldwin, and Earl Haig, Commander of British forces in World War I. In light of the fact that citizenship was conferred on Jones 28 years after he won the Grand Slam, it is somewhat obvious that his exploits on the golf course did not comprise the sole basis for such a singular honor. It is a recognition that Jones was much more than the most distinguished golfer of his era, and, some say, of all time. His record supports the merits of these contentions.

Many people assume that Bob Jones spent his entire life winning championships on the best courses in the world. They believe that Jones must have been carefully groomed by the best teachers and probably practiced like the dickens all his life. They think of him as being like Hogan, who would rather practice than play on the course. Or like Babe Zaharias, who would practice until her hands bled.

Nothing could be further from the truth. Bob Jones never had a formal golf lesson in his life. He was born a sickly child in Atlanta and couldn't get solid food down until about age five. Coincidentally, young Alexa Stirling had the same problems. Both their parents decided to take their ill children to the edge of the East Lake golf course of the Atlanta Athletic Club and turn them out to pasture. At age six, young Rob, as his parents called him, began slipping over the golf course fence and watching Carnoustie professional Stewart Maiden play golf. He carefully studied Maiden's style and then ran home to mimic what he saw using a sawed-off cleek given by Fulton Colville, who belonged to the club. Jones was both a child prodigy and a genius at imitating other golfers. He could get quite a few laughs from imitating the more ridiculous golf swings employed by eccentric East Lake members. As Jones grew up at East Lake, it became obvious he was a gifted athlete. He won the junior club championship at age nine. Two years later, he shot 80 on the tough East Lake course. At 13, he won two tournaments and the club championships at East Lake and Druid Hills. The next year Jones became the youngest ever to qualify for the U.S. Amateur contested at Merion. He was put out in the third round by past champion Robert A. Gardner. He still won four tournaments that year, including the Georgia State Amateur.

But Jones hated to practice. He never had to. If he ever got into trouble, Bob went to the practice tee with Stewart Maiden and got straightened out in less than five minutes. Usually Bob's problem was the ball kept creeping back in his stance. Maiden simply said, "Move the ball up a little. Now hit hell out of it." By the time Jones finished his swing and looked over, Maiden was already halfway back to his shop in the clubhouse.

Jones' friend Alexa was another story. Maiden taught her golf fundamentals from the ground up. She practiced like crazy and followed Maiden's advice to the letter. Her dedication was properly rewarded. By 1916, Alexa won the first of three U.S. Women's Amateur titles. She, not Boy Wonder, was the trailblazer in winning major championships at East Lake.

In the seven lean years from 1916 to 1923, Jones never won a major championship, although he played in five U.S. Amateurs, three U.S. Opens, one British Open, and one British Amateur. He did win half a dozen regional tournaments but wasn't satisfied.

There were three lessons Jones had to learn before the

Jimmy Demaret
By Bernie Fuchs

to be partnered with. He treated you as a fellow conqueror of Old Man Par and not just another adversary who needed a drubbing.

The second lesson Jones learned on his way to the Seven Fat Years was that he deserved to be a champion. It was difficult for Jones because he was a genuinely modest person. His friend and "secret weapon," newspaper writer O.B. Keeler, helped Jones with his confidence. "Son, you're the greatest golfer in the world, and when you get that conviction in your skull, you'll win not one but a lot of them," Keeler told him. It worked like a snake charm. By the time Jones was through, he won 23 of the 52 tournaments he entered. He finished first or second in 11 of 13 U.S. and British Open Championships. He won an astonishing 42% of the major championships he entered (13 of 31). By comparison, Ben Hogan won just 27% of the majors he played (9 of 33). Nicklaus won 18% of his (18 of 100). It is also interesting that Jones was never defeated twice by the same man in competition. These numbers say a lot for confidence.

The third lesson Jones learned before breaking into the world arena was to conquer a fiery temper. As a hot-blooded Southern lad, Jones could swear the most profane adult oaths while heaving his Calamity Jane to kingdom come. In one club-throwing contest during the National Amateur, Jones quipped, "The only reason I won is my opponent was the first to run out of clubs."

Gene Sarazen admitted that he threw clubs too, and Jones wasn't the only offender. But Jones embarrassed himself royally on his inaugural pilgrimage to the British Open Championship in 1921. He was playing well and positioned to receive runner-up amateur honors but for the "most inglorious failure" of his golfing life. His temper got the best of him in the third round. At the short 11th hole, Jones played several strokes in Hill bunker, but he got so mad the ball only came out in his pocket. He then tore up his scorecard and scratched from the tournament. The British press excoriated him for such a sorry display of sportsmanship. They expected more from the young prodigy from America. "Master Bobby is a boy and a rather ordinary boy after all," they wrote. Jones was only beginning to get the picture. Back home, he threw a club toward his bag in anger and it ricocheted into the leg of a woman spectator. Jones received a stern letter from the USGA warning him that his playing privileges would be suspended if it happened again. It never did. Jones resolved not to let his emotions get the best of him in competition.

breakthrough came with his first U.S. Open Championship title in 1923. First, he had to learn to play Old Man Par and not his opponent. Jones initially played every shot for the maximum possible result. "Shoot the works," he called it. Soon he learned that sometimes the safest shot was the best shot. If he ignored his playing partner and played for par, Jones could reduce the stress on his game. Old Man Par never got down in one putt but also never took three. Best to shoot for par and let his opponents shoot for what they could. This strategy actually made Bob a wonderful person

Arnold Palmer
By Walt Spitzmiller

He became thereafter such a model of proper deportment that today the USGA's highest award for sportsmanship is given in his honor. Even with his attitude adjustment, Jones continued to play with determination. "The Times of London" described it best: "He subdued a naturally fiery temper so that outwardly he played the game as a man of ice though inwardly the flames continued to leap up within."

After breaking the ice with his first major victory at the 1923 U.S. Open, Jones soon became the man to beat. All others in both the amateur and professional ranks contracted a disease identified by Gene Sarazen as "Jonesitis." As they passed each other in the adjoining fairways, one golfer hollered to the other, "How's Jones going?" Pretty darn good according to his record. Neither Walter Hagen nor Gene Sarazen ever defeated Jones in any U.S. or British Open Championship contested from 1923 until Jones retired in 1930. Hagen once chewed out his fellow pros, "Every time I

happen to be going badly all the rest of you quit on the job. If we don't stop this lad, he will be walking away with all our championships." That's just what Jones did. But Jones was not content to pile one title on top of another in a mathematical race to the highest total. He knew this type of record was fragile and sooner or later someone would come along and add one more to his aggregate. So Jones conceived of a master plan to create a record that would withstand the test of time. In 1926, Jones set out to win all the majors in the world. He won half of them that year, comprised of the U.S. and British Opens. In 1930, he had only his second chance since he was scheduled to play in Britain. He told no one about his plan, including his best friend, O.B. Keeler. But after he won the British Open, British Amateur, and the U.S. Open, his plan was easy for everyone to see. The oddsmakers put his chances at 50-1 to win the final U.S. Amateur Championship. Bobby Cruickshank placed a bet on Jones and the British bookies paid off $60,000 when Bob won. The

Grand Slam has never been duplicated. Keeler was confident it never would when he wrote, "This victory, the fourth major title in the same season and in the space of four months, has now and for all time entrenched Bobby Jones safely within the 'Impregnable Quadrilateral of Golf,' that granite fortress that he alone could take by escalade, and that others may attack in vain, forever."

In later years, the media recognized the sheer impossibility that anyone could disprove what Keeler wrote. So they redefined a "modern" Grand Slam to comprise all professional major titles, including the Masters, PGA, U.S., and British Opens. Only Hogan has come close with three titles in 1953.

It is astonishing that Jones was able to accomplish so much while only playing golf part-time. From October to April, he put his clubs in the closet and only played himself into shape two weeks before each year's major tournaments. He played usually on weekends and no more frequently than the ordinary club member.

One reason he played so little is that he had other important ambitions in his life. In 1922, he graduated from Georgia Tech with a degree in Mechanical Engineering. Then he entered Harvard where he was conferred a degree in English Literature in 1924. Later he entered Emory Law School and after a year took the bar exam to see how difficult it would be. To his amazement, he passed and wasn't required to complete his degree. He was sworn into the bar and practiced law in his father's law firm. The year before, Jones sold real estate for the Adair Realty Company in Sarasota, Florida. He soon discovered he didn't enjoy selling a little piece of himself every time he sold a golf course homesite, so he took up law as a profession.

Jones also didn't enjoy traveling on the road constantly going to golf tournaments. When he won the Grand Slam in 1930, he was sick of being away from his family, and golf was becoming drudgery rather than fun. He had ambitions other than becoming a golf professional at a time when the purses could not even pay expenses. So he retired to pursue his law practice and several other significant endeavors. First, Jones signed to perform in 18 one-reel films for Warner Brothers entitled "How I Play Golf." They were instantly successful and shown to millions of moviegoers in theaters all over the country. Jones also became a vice president of the A.G. Spalding Company and designed the most technologically advanced clubs then known. The flange used on every

golf club today was a Bobby Jones idea. Jones also teamed with Alister MacKenzie to design the Augusta National Golf Club and to establish the Masters tournament. As if these ventures didn't keep him busy enough, Jones also produced four books and wrote over half-a-million words in golf-related publications.

Through all this, Jones never lost the modesty and charm that had been the features of his personality. He was a hero after five o'clock. Many athletes are specially talented on the field, but after five o'clock, they are miserable human beings. They go home, kick the dog, beat the wife, and are in trouble with the law. Today we excuse these "heroes" and say that their personal lives aren't important.

In contrast, Jones was the same gentleman on the golf course as he was off it after five o'clock. He was the old-fashioned hero longed for even today. He had an uncommonly balanced personality comprised in equal parts of humanity, humor, courtesy, and consideration unmatched in the history of sports.

In addition to being a good man to be partnered with in a tournament, Jones was considerate of all around him. In 1927, he won the British Open Championship trophy for the second consecutive year. The British were understandably upset that the trophy was going to America for the fourth year in a row. Jones was sensitive to this tension and told the crowd in his victory speech that he was not going to take the trophy across the Atlantic but would be pleased if it could remain in the custody of his club, the Royal and Ancient, of which he was proud to be a member. The people wildly applauded and began to call Jones "Our Bobby."

In 1929, Jones tied with Al Espinosa in the U.S. Open and earned a play-off the next day. Knowing that Al would want to go to mass in the morning, Jones spontaneously suggested that the match be delayed to accommodate him. In 1926, Jones was sick to his stomach before the final round of the Open at Scioto. He awakened Dr. Earl Ryan in the wee hours of the dawn to get something to soothe the pain. Twenty years later, Jones knocked on the doctor's door again. Dr. Ryan didn't recognize his former patient. Jones said, "I just wanted to thank you for your kindness extended 20 years ago."

Twice in major championships, Jones called penalties on himself. When praised for this, Jones was disgusted. "There's only one way to play and that is by the rules. You might as well praise a man for not robbing a bank." He never sought to hoard money and overly enrich himself from his fame saying, "You can only eat two eggs a day; you can only wear one suit. All you need is enough to pay your bills and be decent to your friends."

Jones also had a gorgeous sense of humor. He once crumpled a $20 bill and asked his caddy to put it in the bunker beside Walter Hagen's ball in a casual match. Walter reflexively picked up the twenty, put it into his pocket and blasted his ball onto the green. When Jones asked Walter what he made on the hole, Jones replied, "Now, Walter, you really made one more due to the penalty for removing a loose impediment in the bunker." He often told stories on himself. One golfer was explaining to Bob how he made an eagle on a particular hole. "What did you hit?" Bob asked. "I hit a four wood," the member replied. "Why, I've never played more than a nine iron on that hole," Bob observed. "You ever make two?" the member shot back. In 1954, Jones joined Tommy Armour, Gene Sarazen, and Johnny Farrell at Winged Foot in celebration of Jones' victory there in 1929. Joe Dey brought along Calamity Jane, Bob's famous putter, and each player tried to reproduce Jones sinking of the vicious 12-foot putt on the final hole to gain a play-off. All of them but Jones missed from the very spot Jones played the stroke in 1929. Joe Dey then asked Jones if he cared to try. "No thanks," quipped Jones. "I already made it."

In his middle forties, Jones was stricken with a rare neurological disorder that tragically forced him to use a cane, then leg braces, then a wheelchair. He was in constant throbbing pain until the end of his life over 20 years later. Through it all, he never lost his sense of humor and never dwelled on his misfortune. "You play the ball as it lies," Jones said and declined to discuss the subject in public with his closest friends.

Bob's fishing pal, Charlie Elliott, made a special swivel seat so Bob could at least enjoy the water. One day a dock worker who lifted the crippled body of Jones onto the boat couldn't contain himself, saying, "Mr. Jones, pardon me for saying so, but it's hard for me to imagine that you were once the greatest golfer in the world and won the Grand Slam." Jones looked up with a grin and replied softly, "It wasn't easy." In 1954, Jones attended the silver anniversary party for Nashville newpaperman Fred Russell. It was a who's who of sport attended by Red Grange, Jack Dempsey, Gene Tunney, and the Four Horsemen of Notre Dame. Everyone had drinks in a reception room and then walked into the ballroom for dinner. Jones was brought in last to a standing ovation. When the crowd quieted down, Jones raised his glass and

replied, "I presume that little show was because I was the only man smart enough to bring my drink into the room with me." The crack brought the house down.

Despite all the reasons for Jones to puff his chest with pride in public, he never did. Ralph McGill of the "Atlanta Journal" accurately reported, "Jones never took himself or his accomplishments so seriously that he stuffed his shirt with them. Of them all, his feet were freest of clay."

In the early 1960s, writer Charles Price sent Jones the manuscript for a history on his career and asked him to prepare a foreword. Jones replied in his usual modest way, "I only wish I had been that good." In truth and fact, he was.

The American woman golfer whose lofty standards and contributions most closely parallel those of Jones is Babe Zaharias. Her stellar accomplishments were not wholly uninspired by singular efforts of earlier women like Alexa Stirling and Glenna Collett. Alexa was an extraordinary lady of myriad talents other than golf. She could repair a car engine, manufacture furniture, and play concert violin. But she also could play golf like few others. Alexa won the U.S. Women's Amateur three consecutive years in 1916, 1919, and 1920. (The championship was suspended during World War I.) She won the Southern Women's Amateur three times (1915, 1916, 1920) and the Canadian Women's Amateur twice (1920, 1934). During the First World War, Alexa joined Bobby Jones as the "Dixie Whiz Kids" toured the United States playing exhibition matches with professionals and raising over $150,000 for the Red Cross.

One young girl who was inspired by Alexa's play was Glenna Collett. "I succumbed to her influence the first time I saw her play," Glenna said. Glenna prospered under the tutelage of Alex Smith, who knew how championships are won. He twice collected the U.S. Open, in 1904 and 1910. Before this student was through, Glenna would win a record six U.S. Women's Amateur Championships. To that total, she added four victories in the North and South Amateur. Her fluid style and rhythmic swing was often compared to that of Jones.

Perhaps the greatest female athlete in history, Mildred Didrikson Zaharias, was all this, indeed, and even more. That special woman whom people would come to regard with great affection as "Babe" (after baseball's immortal hero) set out in her teens "to be the greatest athlete that ever lived."

Since childhood, Babe had the urge to get into sports. Her parents were Norwegian. Father Ole was a seafarer and traveled around the Cape Horn 17 times. Her mother was a

Jack Nicklaus
By Walt Spitzmiller

natural athlete, talented in both ice skating and skiing in Norway. Babe's father once made a set of skis for her mother out of barrel staves so she could go to town and run her errands. On one of Poppa's trips to Port Arthur, Texas, he decided it was the place to raise his family. So to Texas it was for Babe and her family.

Born after twins, Mildred was called "Min Babe" (my best girl). She was followed by younger brother Arthur ("Bubba"). Her name was switched after Mildred began hitting home runs in baseball games. She then was forever referred to as "Babe."

Babe was put through the athletic paces by her childhood friends and her mother. Her formative days were filled with both wholesome and somber memories. A big day was traveling on horse and wagon to pick blackberries as fast as possible so that the remaining day could be filled with fun playing in sawdust piles as big as a house.

Babe was always delegated the chore of "running" to the store on last minute errands. Of course, she ran the entire way there and back, prompting the remark, "Why, you only just left." Once, Babe was on her way to get hamburger and stopped to watch a ball game in the schoolyard. The next thing she knew, Babe found herself playing with the other children. Over an hour passed. When Mama came around to see what had happened, a dog was finishing the remains of the hamburger. Mama ran fast to discipline her daughter, but Babe was able to keep ahead of her. Babe learned an important lesson in life: "Don't mess with Mama."

Babe's neighborhood had seven hedges between her house and the corner grocery. On her way to the store, Babe practiced jumping those hedges. One was higher than the rest, so Babe successfully persuaded that neighbor to cut the hedge into conformity. Babe's sister Lillie ran with her but didn't bother with jumping the hedges as she ran. Babe's unusual style of "crooking" her left knee to get over the two-foot-thick hedges stayed with her even into the Olympics, although the coaches tried to modify that style to accommodate the smaller one and three quarter-inch-thick hurdle.

Babe always had the urge to do things better than everybody else, no matter if academic or athletic in nature. She was expert in sewing her own clothes and bubbled with

Babe Zaharias
By Walt Spitzmiller

excitement when she won Texas State Fair ribbons with her special designs.

The dream of achieving the distinction of "greatest athlete ever" was nurtured in no small part by Babe's father Ole, the Norwegian seafarer. Ole read to his children about sports in the newspapers and talked about the famous golfers like Bobby Jones, Walter Hagen, Joyce Wethered, and Glenna Collett. Papa Ole spoke enthusiastically of the 1928 Olympics in Amsterdam, Holland, and the "stars" who competed. Babe, only 14, buoyed by the thought of crossing the ocean, announced to her father that she would compete in the Olympics the following year. Only then did her father explain that the Olympics were held every four

years. Her training began immediately.

The initial challenge was presented by basketball in Beaumont, Texas, junior and senior high schools. After a few barefooted lessons from the school coach after hours, and a lot of practice, Babe was leading scorer in her first starts. Babe was soon "discovered" by the Dallas talent agent for the Employer Casualty Company, which sponsored women's amateur athletic teams that competed nationally. Colonel M.J. McCoombs coached these teams to a second-place finish in the Women's AAU Tournament in 1927. It was a business and athletic relationship, which would last for years and benefit both. Babe could type 86 words a minute and use a slide rule. She also was the leading scorer in her first outing while defeating the defending national champions. In fact, Babe was an All-American basketball player three years in a row beginning in 1930. She scored over 100 points in one game against lesser competition on the way to a national championship in 1931.

Colonel McCoombs clearly had an eye for talent. After basketball season ended in 1931, he asked Babe if she would like to see a track meet. While on the infield, Babe asked the Colonel what that "long" thing was? That's a "javelin," came the reply, replete with a demonstration by the Colonel of its use.

Never one to miss an opportunity, Babe made several attempts but only managed to raise several welts on her back when the javelin "slapped" it. The Colonel also showed the Babe what reminded her of the "hedge jumping" she had done back home in Texas. What she knew as hedges were now called "hurdles." The high jump was also demonstrated. The whole track meet reminded Babe of her vow to participate in the Olympics. Both the Colonel and Babe talked the president of Employer Casualty into organizing and sponsoring a track team for summer events. Babe announced she would enter all ten events. Though some laughed, she did win eight of ten events in one meet after a rigorous training program. The high jump presented a special challenge. Babe initially used the "scissors"-style jump technique until she reached the women's world record. Then she realized that the "western roll" was the best style to break the record. It is required only that the feet go over the bar first.

Babe won the javelin throw and baseball throw in the 1930 Women's National AAU Championships. Her newly set world record in the broad jump was bettered by Stella Walsh by a quarter-inch. In the 1931 championships, Babe won three firsts: the baseball throw (296 feet), the broad jump, and the 80-meter hurdles (12 sec. flat). These events were a warm-up to the 1932 Olympics in Los Angeles. Olympic contestants were chosen as the winners in the national championships. Babe would be the only woman in history to win a national championship single-handedly. She was advised that this was possible by entering eight of ten possible events for Employer Casualty. She dropped only the 50-yard and 220-yard dashes. Babe received quite a roar from the crowd when announced as "the team." She won first-place finishes in the shotput, baseball throw, javelin (world record), 80 meter hurdle (world record), and high jump (tie). Babe got "blanked" in the 100-meter dash, placed fourth in the discus.

Out of eight entries, Babe placed first in five events, tied for first in the sixth, and won the national championship all by herself. Commentators reported this was "the most amazing series of performances ever accomplished by any individual, male or female, in track history."

Babe went on to enter three of five possible women's events in the Olympics – javelin, high jump, and hurdles.

On her train ride to the 1932 Los Angeles Olympics, Babe daily ran the length of the train. She trained in the aisles. When she arrived in Los Angeles, she was compelled to resist her coach's insistence that she change her technique in the hurdles and javelin throw.

On her first attempt in 1932, Babe threw a new world and Olympic record in the javelin. She also tore a cartilage on the throw, which did not permit her to better the effort on the two additional tries. Never one to complain, she kept news of the injury to herself. She won the finals of the 80-meter hurdles after causing a false start. Only the high jump remained for a clean sweep. She attempted a "western roll" and although she cleared the bar, the judges disallowed the jump while claiming Babe's feet failed to cross the bar first. Later photos tend to prove Babe's point. It was quite a controversial call, and the sports commentators had a field day with it.

Sports columnist Grantland Rice was one who commiserated with Babe about the bum ruling. He generously invited Babe for a golf game after the Olympics. This game changed women's golf history.

Babe had been introduced to golf by Colonel McCoombs, who took her to a driving range in Dallas for a few shots. Her initial drives were perfect – about 250 yards. She broke the club, however, standing too close to a light pole on her follow-through. The Scotsman who ran the driving range was more excited about the distance of the shot than the broken club. The golf match with Grantland Rice, and with noted authors Paul Gallico, Braven Dyer, and Westbrook Pegler, was Babe's first true golf outing. Rice and Babe stood the other three since Rice was the best player of them all. Babe's drives that day were between 240 and 260 yards as she recorded an 86. Rice and the Babe prevailed over their opponents but not without some gamesmanship. Gallico hit his best tee shot to the short 16th. Babe then bet Paul she could footrace him to the green, and he accepted the challenge. Arriving winded at the green, Gallico then four-putted and that ended the match. Babe definitely got the golf bug.

Babe's return to Dallas from the 1932 Olympics was not

received differently from the reception provided to Charles Lindberg on his Atlantic crossing or to Bobby Jones in 1926 and 1930. She reveled in the parades and interviews and appearances. She also burned with desire to be a competitive golfer. Although she was careful to decline gifts that would compromise her amateur standing, an unauthorized photo endorsement of a 1932 Dodge cost Babe her amateur status. The AAU (Amateur Athletic Union) reversed itself later, but Babe decided to turn pro anyway. Chrysler Dodge hired Babe to attract customers at auto shows with her personality and her ability to play harmonica. Babe also performed in a comical theatrical act at the Chicago Palace Theater, demonstrating various athletic feats: hurdling, running a treadmill, hitting golf shots, and, of course, playing the harmonica. The reviews were good but Babe left that stage for a more important one to her - championship golf.

After a short stint playing pro basketball and billiard exhibitions, Babe dedicated her talent solely to golf in the summer of 1933. A driving range pro, Stan Kertes, gave her free lessons day and night until her room and board bankroll ran out. Babe then toured in 1934 with a pro basketball team called Babe Didrikson's All-Americans. She became pals with Jack Dempsey, Babe Ruth, and Dizzy Dean. She then toured with the "House of David" baseball team, doing exhibition pitching.

In 1934 Babe entered her first golf tournament - the Fort Worth Women's Invitational. She was low medalist with 77 but was put out of the subsequent match play. She next took aim at the 1935 Texas State Women's Open Championship.

In those days there was no professional women's golf tour. Babe would later join others to found the LPGA in 1949. She practiced until her hands became bloody and sore. She then taped them and practiced until there was blood all over the tape. At night she schooled herself on the rules. She once disqualified herself in 1946 for hitting the wrong ball. "You have to play by the rules of golf, just as you have to live by the rules of life. There's no other way," she reasoned.

Babe won a dramatic victory over Peggy Chandler in the finals to capture the Texas championship. She then set her sights on the national championship. However, the USGA reversed itself and ruled that Babe was a professional, not an amateur. She was ineligible. Rather than cry about it, Babe signed on with the Goldsmith Sons (later McGregor) Sporting Goods Company. She played exhibitions with Gene Sarazen It was not uncommon for her to unleash 300-yard drives. She once hit a drive 346 yards in favorable conditions. Unlike the graceful English star Joyce Wethered, Babe was a slugger. Herbert Warren Wind said the "explanation was that she took the club back on the outside as she rocked into her swing, and then brought it directly up; as her hands moved down and through the ball from that position, she never allowed her right hand to cross over her left." No matter how hard she hit the ball she could not hook it.

On the tours with Sarazen, Babe had a bag full of trick shots. She became a master at wisecracking with the galleries and they loved her. She simultaneously received invaluable lessons from Sarazen, the master. He taught Babe the bunker shot and much more about the mental side of the game.

In 1938, at 23, Babe entered the Los Angeles Open. Although it was a men's tournament, there was no prohibition for ladies to play. Babe shot 84. True, she failed to win the tournament, but she did meet and later marry her playing partner, professional wrestler George Zaharias.

During early 1939, George and Babe toured Australia. Babe wowed the Aussie crowds with her outgoing personality and by shooting within one stroke of the score posted by the reigning Australian men's champion. One writer commented at the time: "The plain fact is that Miss Didrikson is a vastly better golfer than Miss Helen Hicks, Miss Pam Barton or any other woman we have seen. She can hit a ball farther than all except a very few men. At Victoria the day was bitterly cold, the turf was thick and dead, and generally it was a perfect day for a test for anyone to endure. Here are some of the genuine and checked figures, with turf not helping the least and over level ground. She hit drives of 230, 245 and 250 yards in the first three holes. She hit her first mashie 170 yards and another 180 yards. In bunkers her class was that of Sarazen. Her approach work from 140 to 30 yards from the green was not completely finished and she was good but not overly impressive on the greens. If Miss Didrikson tightens up her short game, she may get a place among the best men professionals in golf."

In 1940, Babe applied to the USGA for reinstatement as an amateur. A three-year wait was required. She forwent prize money while playing and winning ladies majors such as the Western Women's Open. Then while waiting out the amateur grace period, Babe took up tennis in her usual "all out" style. She took lessons from the best instructor, Eleanor Tennant, and applied for entry into the Pacific Southwest Championships but was politically rejected as a "professional" once again. Without the challenge of tournament competition in tennis, Babe turned to bowling

Mickey Wright   Patty Berg   Nancy Lopez   Kathy Whitworth

By Walt Spitzmiller

and, of course, kept up her golf. She played with Sam Snead, Bob Hope, Bing Crosby, Byron Nelson, and Ben Hogan among the top names. Her strategy was to sharpen her game with the better men players. The tournament schedule was abbreviated during the war years so any competition was welcomed.

Babe's amateur status was finally restored in 1943. She won a bushel of California tournaments, including the Midwinter Women's Championship with a double eagle.

She added the 1944 Western Women's Open and successfully defended her title in 1945, even with the news that her mother had passed away before the final round. Also in 1945 Babe won her second Texas Women's Open title. The Associated Press awarded her the Woman Athlete of the Year honor for 1945, which she added to the same honor bestowed in the 1932 Olympic year. Before she finished, the Associated Press gave her six such awards, together with the Woman Athlete of the Half Century in 1950.

In 1946, the war over, tournament golf resumed full swing. Babe then began a string of victories that would extend to 17 in a row. (Byron Nelson won only 11.) After two victories at Tam O'Shanter Country Club in Michigan (the All American and World Championship), Babe took her first Women's National Amateur Championship at Southern Hills in Tulsa against fierce competition. Babe kept adding victories in 1946 and 1947 against the likes of Helen Hicks and Louise Suggs. At Augusta, she won the Titleholders Tournament, which was little sister to the Masters. After consecutive win number 15, Babe's husband George suggested she try her luck in Britain in the style of Bobby

Jones' Grand Slam. Babe waffled until her instructor Tommy Armour, finally persuaded her to go to the 1947 British Women's Amateur, more properly the "Ladies Amateur Golf Championship Tournament under the Management of the Ladies Golf Union." An American had never won it until Babe beat all the competitors at Gullane, Scotland, that year. Babe warmed up to the Scots immediately despite some controversy that the American was "jinxed" against winning. She wore kilts and mingled at tea with the townspeople and won them over with her charm and lack of guile. After conquering her opponent soundly in one match, Babe suggested they play the bye holes for fun. To the delight of the spectators, that's just what they did. She sometimes performed trick shots learned in exhibitions: "I gave them some of the trick shots I use in exhibitions in this country. There's one where I put a kitchen match on the ground behind my ball on the tee, and when I drive, it sounds like a small cannon being fired, because that match goes off with a loud pop. I did that off the seventeenth tee, and the ball sailed nearly 300 yards out there and landed in a trap right in front of the green. From the trap I did another of my stunts. I balanced one ball on top of the other, which is a trick in itself. I swing, and the bottom ball is supposed to go on the green and the top one into my pocket. Well, not only did the one ball jump into my pocket, the other went right into the hole."

Babe's friendly reputation had preceded her. When she mentioned to the press that she owned few winter clothes, the people began sending packages that stacked up in the hotel lobby. The townspeople were enchanted with the American.

During a practice round, Babe chipped a bone in her thumb while hacking a shot from what she called the deep "winds" (whins or gorse). She kept the public from this knowledge by wearing a glove over the bandage so as to prevent talk of an excuse for losing. This actually worked to her benefit since it prevented her from "slugging" the ball in her usual style. As a result, she missed only one fairway the entire tournament. Even so, on the par five 15th hole (540 yards) Babe reached the green with a driver and four iron assisted by only a slight breeze. In the early rounds, Babe "took practically all the spectators" (5,000 - 8,000) and crashed her way over the hills and dales, "tore holes in the rough with tremendous recovery shots," and won with "the most tremendous exhibition of long driving ever seen in women's golf." She interrupted the usual "quietness" of golf by asking the crowd to be noisy so she'd play better. During the finals, Babe put her arms around two kilted Scotsmen in the gallery and asked if they would like her to knock her wedge shot into the hole. They assented with a typical Scottish burr, and Babe almost fully complied while leaving the ball only on the lip of the cup. Upon winning the final match, Babe donned her Stewart tartan kilt and delighted the crowd by performing the Highland Fling.

Babe received a heroine's welcome complete with rose parade in Denver upon return to the United States. She followed her return with a 17th straight victory at the Broadmoor Match Play Tournament in Colorado Springs, while retiring the cup in the process.

The lure of professional golf and lucrative exhibition offers opened a second professional career for Babe in 1947. Her streak of 17 straight ended at the Texas Women's Open that year. But in the next tournament she set a new world's record of 293 for women in 72 holes of play. She boldly applied for the Men's U.S. Open, but the USGA rejected her application. Then she won the 1948 National Women's Open and was leading money winner with $3,400.

The problem of too-few women's pro tournaments was solved in 1949 when the Ladies Professional Golf Association (LPGA) was founded by Babe, Patty Berg, Hope Seignious, and several others, including the president of Wilson Sports (L.B. Iceley) and promoter Fred Corcoran. The total tournament purse of $15,000 in 1949 soon grew to $200,000 in 1955.

Babe again led the money title from 1949 to 1951, along with 11 victories and the National Open title in 1950. She was slowed by a hernia operation in 1952. Her recuperation was not followed by the usual "all out" style of golf. She thought her fatigue might be rectal cancer but didn't tell anyone until her doctor revealed the secret in 1953.

Babe underwent a permanent colostomy. She "left it in the hands of God" and accepted her condition while serving selflessly as a fundraiser for the Cancer Society. She consoled other cancer and colostomy patients who were scared about surgery and all that inevitably followed. Her courage was steadfast, and she never gave up hope even after 43 days in the hospital.

Two months after her surgery, Babe played nine holes, shooting 37. Three and a half months later saw Babe hit a 250-yard drive off the first tee of the Tam O'Shanter All American Tournament. She finished 15th, then third in another tournament the following week, after leading the third round.

By 1954, Babe was back, but she was asking herself the same question as the public, "Could she win again?" That question was positively answered with a victory over Patty Berg in February 1954 in the Serbin Women's Open. Following the win, Babe dined in the White House with Ike to promote the Cancer Crusade. She thereafter overcame all odds to win the 1954 National Women's Open by 12 shots over Betty Hicks. The Associated Press voted her the Female Athlete of the Year for the sixth time.

Babe continued winning tournaments through 1955. When asked why she didn't just take it easy, she explained: "One reason is that every time I get out and play well in a golf tournament, it seems to buck up people with the same cancer trouble I had. I can tell that from the letters I keep getting .... Another reason why I've kept coming back to the golf circuit is that I helped start the Ladies Professional Golf Association, and I want to help it keep on growing."

Babe won the Peach Blossom Betsy Rawls Tournament in the summer of 1955 before undergoing surgery for a ruptured disc. This was followed by news that the cancer had returned for a second match. She never lost her hope and was courageous to the end when she died in 1956 at the age of 42.

Not all that has been said about Babe is complimentary. She sometimes exploited her prima donna stardom. Patty Berg remembered: "She was also adamant about not playing preferred lies, no matter how bad course conditions were.... She'd just say to the sponsor, 'Move those tees back or Ah'm withdrawing from the tournament. And then see how you get your galleries.' Just like that. Same way with winter rules. Babe didn't like them. She'd say after she won, 'I still think we shoulda played 'em as they laid.' Oh, she was something else."

Of all her accomplishments there is one that stands above the rest and may never be equaled or exceeded. It was not the 19 records she set in track and field. It was not the two gold and one silver medal in the 1932 Olympics. Nor was it the 31 professional wins in golf, including three U.S. Women's Opens. It wasn't the victory as the first American ever to win the British Ladies Championship or founding the Ladies Professional Golf Association. It wasn't even the athletic versatility that permitted her to excel at every sport she attempted. Rather, her ultimate accomplishment is that Babe mastered the game of life in a courageous and sometimes selfless "all out" style befitting a genuine champion.

On rare occasions, we chance to meet people whose extraordinary gifts stand apart from the crowd. Like a comet streaking across the heavens, these people make such an indelible impression upon us that we cannot forget them despite our proclivity to do so. Sometimes we choose to lose our fantasies and "live" through such heroes and heroines, especially when the realization hits home that we may never rise above comfortable mediocrity. These rare people are invariably characterized not only by the tremendous physical achievements against all odds, but also by the superior inner strengths of spirit and selfless striving for perfection. They are the authors of the American golf legacy.

| Morris | MacKenzie | Tillinghast | Ross | Thomas |

The Early Legends of Golf Course Design
By Paul Milosevich

Fine Art of America's Fairways

East

5th Hole - Number 2
By Linda Hartough

Pinehurst
PINEHURST, NC

It is said about Pinehurst, "Golf is not a matter of life and death here. It's more important than that."

Ben Hogan won his first professional championship here. Chick Evans, Walter Hagen, Tommy Armour, Bobby Jones, Babe Zaharias, Gene Sarazen, Byron Nelson, Sam Snead, Gary Player, Jack Nicklaus, Arnold Palmer, Tom Watson, Ben Crenshaw, and Hale Irwin are just some of the greats who have sung the praises of golf at Pinehurst.

Today Pinehurst Resort consists of eight golf courses, but there are 30-plus more within a 15 mile radius designed and created by the greatest names in American golf course architecture: Ellis Maples, Robert Trent Jones, Rees Jones, Tom Fazio, Jack Nicklaus, Arnold Palmer, and the grandfather of golf course design, Donald Ross.

In 1895, Pinehurst's founder James Tufts of the American Soda Fountain Company purchased 5,000 acres of barren sandhills for $7,500. He installed a lackluster nine-hole layout in 1898.

Pinehurst may be synonymous with golf, but it is also much more than golf. North Carolina's sandhills, Pinehurst's locale, have long been known for the healing qualities of their soft southern air. Tufts considered it an ideal spot for a health spa and residential colony for escapees from the sooty, cold environs of northeastern cities. Frederick Olmsted, the landscape architect who designed New York's Central Park, was commissioned to design the village of Pinehurst, which has since gained a place in history as one of the country's first planned communities.

Pinehurst was unusual from the beginning because it took a reverse approach as not arranged according to the expedient rule of "form follows function." Instead, Olmsted took the scenic route "with open park spaces and winding streets that attain their usefulness by following lines of beauty." The compound was charted with winding pedestrian paths that created a gracious, unhurried air and contributed to neighborliness. The stately trees which grace Pinehurst today were nonexistent then, but as the resort developed, it was reforested with every species of plant and shrub that would take hold in the thin soil. In the springtime, Pinehurst is a cloud of red and pink as its azaleas and rhododendrons open the season with a profusion of blossoms. At all times, Pinehurst's vegetation is so carefully cultivated it could easily serve as a botanical garden.

At the central village green, rather than at the community outskirts, Olmsted placed several inns, a casino, schoolhouse, general store, individual cottages, and grounds for the traditional sports of the day. This placement brought the residents together rather than dispersing them, and an attitude of friendliness is still at least to some degree the legacy of its well-conceived design. It has a timeless character once described this way:

"Pinehurst people don't try to outdo each other with homes – they don't drive golf carts with dry bars or Rolls Royce grilles. They have no use for neon signs, bus tours, fat farms, night clubs, stretch limos, outsized swimming pools, art galleries that insult your taste, antique shops full of bric-a-brac made a week ago, restaurants that award themselves three stars, or any of the rest of the confetti with which other golf resorts today carnivalize themselves."

Golf is carefully cultivated at Pinehurst, which is ranked by the experts as one of the top ten destinations for the sport worldwide. Golf had made its debut in the

5th Hole - Number 8
By Noble Powell

United States little more than a decade earlier (1888), and its appeal was instantly evident.

In 1901, Tufts convinced a young Scotsman, Donald Ross, to join him in Pinehurst. Ross was from Dornoch, Scotland, where in 1893 he was a greenkeeper and professional. He had studied club-making under Robert Forgan, and greenkeeping and the duties of a golf professional under the legendary Old Tom Morris in St. Andrews. Upon arriving in Pinehurst, Ross immediately set about to rebuild and expand Number One.

From the outset, Ross put his indelible stamp on Pinehurst, their reputations intertwining as they grew together. Ross' philosophy was to work with the natural landscape rather than to fight it. If an architect were to approach North Carolina's sand hills today with the assignment of creating a golf course, massive machinery and power would be available to bulldoze, move, and grade acres of earth; pump in millions of gallons of water; and irrigate miles of lawn. Ross had only brawny teams of mules and men at his disposal. Perhaps that limitation reinforced his natural reluctance to undertake dramatic reconstruction of natural terrain.

Ross' first challenge, however, meant significant change to the landscape he had been given to work with. There was not a single blade of grass at Pinehurst when Ross arrived there. Neither tees nor greens were the lush affairs they are today; instead, hard-packed clay served as the launch point for the first drive. Sand greens were smoothed over by rags tied onto a broom handle. Ross' work may have seemed less daunting to him because in Scotland the word "links" means "sandy stretches of country near the sea." He was, at least,

working with familiar conditions. For example, it was not until 1936 that the sand greens were successfully converted to Bermuda grass.

In 1903, Pinehurst's now legendary Number Two was unveiled. Ross always considered Number Two his masterpiece, and when he designed it, he determined to create the finest golf course in the South. Throughout his life he tinkered with the layout, making little improvements here and there until 1935, when he completed a fairly deep renovation. In 1946, Ross remodeled one more hole on Number Two, the last alteration he would make in his bid for perfection.

Ross designed two more courses for Pinehurst: Number Three in 1910 and Number Four in 1919. Much of his original work remains, continuing to offer classic beauty and challenge. Pinehurst claims that 13 of the holes on Number Two have remained virtually unchanged since 1923. It is high praise for Pinehurst that they were wise enough to let Ross' work stand the test of time.

Extreme golf course design ruled the sport for a time, but like most fads, the staying power just wasn't there. Today many critics recognize that golf is coming full circle, and they say that Number Two is "where the game has been and where it is going." Quality tells, and the pendulum is swinging back to the principles of "deceptive simplicity" always practiced by Donald Ross.

Ross' trademarks included tightly enveloped fairways marked by difficult combinations of angles; small greens contoured with dips and swales; and torturous approaches guarded with bunkers, ridges, and hollows that appear innocent from a distance. Unsuspecting Pinehurst golfers perceive simplicity in the lack of drama and are lulled into a false sense of security. Then, once hooked, they are confounded with choices and possibilities that create infinite approaches to each shot. This quiet greatness produces a different game each time the course is encountered. Rather than relying on a single sensational element that overwhelms, golf here builds on components carefully designed to understate and surprise.

Ross held the distinction of being the first-full time course designer in America. He went on to design 450-500 courses – so many that the exact numbers elude even historians.

After Ross' death in 1948, other world-class designers added their own legacies to his. Ellis Maples designed Number Five in 1961, incorporating a number of water hazards and creating the famous "Cathedral Hole" that features a pond encircled by a stand of ancient pines. Number Six was added in 1979, designed by Tom Fazio, and quickly recognized as Pinehurst's toughest course. Rees Jones allowed the wetlands and underbrush to foil golfers on Number Seven, which he designed in 1986. In 1997, Fazio was invited back to design The Centennial,

Pinehurst's Number Eight. He paid homage to Pinehurst's history, creating The Centennial in the spirit of Number Two, as a tribute to purists who seek to experience the game for the sheer sport of it. Club Corporation of America, its management, and staff on-site have all carried out the mandate to "simply let it be the best golf resort in the world."

Pinehurst's appeal has survived the upheavals of the past century, in part because it remained true to its classic values. Its changes have been subtle, bringing in the best of the new while keeping the best of the old. Because it has matured under scrupulous respect for its tradition, Pinehurst is all the things that embody the American tradition of Southern beauty: soft-spoken, gracious, well-mannered, aware of the world but somehow beyond its reach. It has never lost the qualities of leisure, repose, and hospitality that its founder envisioned.

Many great competitions both amateur (The North & South) and professional have been held at Pinehurst, and in 1999, the U. S. Open Championship will be contested over the fabled Number Two Course. It just does not get much better than Pinehurst.

9th Hole - Number 7
By Adriano Manocchia

Pinehurst

There are other spots on this gracious earth,
*   where the sky is just as blue,*
There are haunts made fine by the stalwart pine,
*   where the charms of a June are known,*
But I've learned today in a curious way why Pinehurst
*   stands alone.*

There are gardens fair in the sunny South
*   where the rich magnolias bloom,*
There are fairy scenes with their wealth of greens,
*   and the scent of a sweet perfume,*
But more than a sky where the sun shines high,
*   and more than a ridge of pine,*
Or a sea or a lake, God needs to make an earthly
*   Golfer's shrine.*

The Lord has lavished his treasures rich
*   all over the orb of earth,*
Yet some are base with the commonplace,
*   and some are lost to mirth,*
But Pinehurst holds in its friendly folds
*   the lure of an honest grip,*
And a manhood fine adds to its gifts divine
*   the wealth of its fellowship.*

It isn't the pine with its towering fronds
*   upraised to the God on high,*
Or the fragrant air that men come to share,
*   and it isn't alone the sky.*
It's the handclasp true, that they seek anew,
*   and the smile on the cheery lip.*
And they come again to be care-free men
*   in a brotherly fellowship.*

Here honor counts more than the victory,
*   and a man is more than his gold;*
Here love of the game means more than the fame,
*   or the joy that the pride may hold.*
Oh, Pinehurst gleams with the finest dreams,
*   and the best that we mortals know,*
It is rich in the things that a true life brings,
*   God grant you may keep it so.*

Edgar A. Guest

18th Hole
By Gordon Wheeler

"I knew that the spectacular view from behind the 18th green at
Wild Dunes would be the inspiration for one of my finest works. But how could
I get the right angle and height? Who knew that the gentleman who just
happened to join Mike Ventola and myself for our picture-taking round lived in a
home with a balcony overlooking the 18th green? Thanks for the help and
hospitality, doctor."   *Artist Gordon Wheeler*

Wild Dunes
ISLE OF PALMS, SC

How many golf clubs can boast of an 18th hole that has the Atlantic Ocean as its water hazard? Not many, making Wild Dunes such a glorious find. Nestled on the northernmost tip of Isle of Palms, Wild Dunes is one of South Carolina's premier oceanfront resorts. It wasn't long ago, however, that these 1600 acres were home to Indians who roamed the island to hunt and fish, and to pirates who, legend has it, buried vast treasures beneath ancient oak trees. One visit to Wild Dunes will quickly reveal that the real treasure isn't buried at all. Landscape as lush as velvet, golden rays of sunlight dancing on the water creating thousands of dazzling jewels, stately oaks, aromatic breezes – these are without a doubt a natural fortune and a prize for all golfers.

World-renowned course architect Tom Fazio was given a picture-perfect setting on which to design Wild Dunes. Just as artist Gordon Wheeler captured the beauty and essence of the 18th hole on canvas, Fazio sculpted and painted fairways, greens, sands, and water with exquisite care, taking pride in protecting the land. And, as usual with any Fazio designed course, the world took notice. Wild Dunes' Links Course began receiving accolades almost immediately upon completion in 1980, becoming a world-ranked course by "Golf Magazine" within 18 months. Just a short drive from the quaint charm of historic Charleston, the beauty begins before you even reach the resort. As you drive over the causeway and up beautiful Isle of Palms, where nature's

splendid hues abound, a feeling of serenity begins to soothe the senses and to melt away the stresses of everyday life. It is no wonder that "Golf Magazine" also awarded Wild Dunes The Gold Medal in 1988, placing it among the Top 12 Golf Resorts in America.

In addition to its colorful panorama, Wild Dunes boasts quite a colorful history. During the Revolutionary War, Lord Cornwallis' command of 2000 soldiers landed on the spot that is now the famed 18th hole, planning to attack Fort Moultrie from the rear. However, American troops did not allow them to "play through," and the land was protected. Perhaps they should have brought their "sticks" instead of rifles? A century later, when war divided the North and South, the Confederate submarine "H.L. Hunley" launched the world's first successful submarine attack in battle off the coast of Isle of Palms, when it rammed the Union warship, "U. S. S. Housatonic," which sank immediately. The ship's sunken remains are still located nearby, and the anchor belonging to the "Housatonic" stands in monument outside the Reception Center at Wild Dunes.

The early 1980s brought the development of a second Tom Fazio-designed golf course, the Harbor Course, making the resort even better and bringing it increased recognition as a premier destination for families, golf enthusiasts, and anyone wishing to experience the beauty and splendor of a world-class resort. At about the same time, the United States Tennis Association selected Wild Dunes as the site of the U. S. Men's Clay Court Championships, propelling the resort to the pinnacle of success in all areas. Known for housing some of the finest tennis amenities available anywhere, "Tennis Magazine" ranked Wild Dunes as one of the Top 50 Tennis Resorts in the Country. The resort proudly maintained this prestigious award for more than a decade. Then, tragically, Mother Nature delivered a devastating blow. On September 21, 1989, Hurricane Hugo, one of the most destructive hurricanes ever to strike the United States, passed directly over Isle of Palms. Wild Dunes was closed for over nine months, amidst near disaster. But strong at heart, she weathered the storm and not only survived, but managed to flourish. Today Wild Dunes proudly reigns as a testament to resiliency.

As you approach the 18th tee, breathing in the beauty around you, realizing the depths of history steeped in the land, you may find it difficult to concentrate on your golf shot.

Live Oak
By Gordon Wheeler

4th Hole - Seaside
By Adriano Manocchia

"As my wife Teresa and I stood looking at the marsh, fairways, and ocean, the landscape slowly turned into a magnificent palette of warm, rich colors. I moved from spot to spot trying to capture it on film. The magic lasted briefly, several minutes, and it was gone. It remains to this day one of the most powerful landscapes I have painted."   *Artist Adriano Manocchia*

Sea Island
SEA ISLAND, GA

Avenue of the Oaks
By Adriano Manocchia

Of the golf courses in Georgia, only Augusta National's Magnolia Lane resonates with a richer tradition than Sea Island's Avenue of the Oaks as a gateway to a magical setting for the game of golf. Perfectly aligned rows of massive, moss-laden water oaks stand sentry over a stretch of graveled lane that ushers a visitor back through time when gracious Southern living and mannered courtliness were the only standard.

The Sea Island resort, a 36-hole golf facility, owned and managed by the Alfred W. Jones family's Sea Island Co. since 1927, is that journey into a world of natural beauty, graceful manner, and world-class amenities that most assuredly includes incomparable golf. St. Simon's Island, the five-mile long barrier island off the southern coast of Georgia that is home to the Sea Island Golf Club, derives its beauty from the abundant marshland landscape that melds with the sea to form the famous "low-country" composition unique to the southeastern United States.

Its grace and Southern charm fairly drip from the limbs of the live oaks' hanging moss with the effect of slowing the living pace to a sociable, Southern saunter. In the shade of those oaks, partial ruins of cotton plantation buildings dating to 1790 are reminders of the property's origins, as is an old cemetery, containing the graves of former residents and slaves, that sits astride a golf hole and is accorded sacred deference. This swampy island landscape, with its innumerable watery inlets and thick reeded grasses, has also inspired the poetry of Sidney Lanier and enticed visits from international royalty and American presidents alike. And when they visited, the 262-room, five-star Cloister Hotel accommodated them. In addition to its copious amenities, Cloister guests are given use of the beach club, which provides miles of private beach access.

But unmistakably, golf is the centerpiece of Sea Island. The original 18 holes, completed by 1929 as separate nine-hole projects, were assessed by no less an authority than Bobby Jones as "one of the world's finest" golf courses after he established the course record of 67 in 1930 – a record that stood for 20 years.

The first nine holes, finished in 1927, is the Plantation course and was a collaboration of Walter Travis and the English tandem of Colt and Alison. A Rees Jones refurbishing in 1992 helped restore original dimensions to bunkers and greens which had been robbed of their contours over the years by Atlantic winds and rains.

The Colt-Alison team, whose work includes England's storied Sunningdale Golf Club in suburban London, finished the Seaside nine two years later. It is generally regarded as the premier layout of the four separate nines, owing that distinction both to the skills of the architects and to its proximity to the ocean. Its fourth and seventh holes in particular represent the essence of the low-country, oceanside golf experience. They maneuver past intimidating marshy hazards on a long journey to their respective greens, but then deliver the payoff with a stunning panorama of the ocean's vastness.

As splendid as that layout remains, and as integral as it was to the establishment of Sea Island's reputation for quality, the resort reached a new level in 1960 with the opening of the Retreat nine created by Dick Wilson. With most of the available ocean-bordering land for golf already in use, Wilson's challenge to match his forebears' artistry was formidable. But the inland routing through thick forest that he carved has proved a worthy furtherance of the standard set by his predecessors. Retreat contains what is considered one of the best par threes in the state in the 180-yard second hole. A right fronting pond and large solitary oak looming to the left leave no bailout option for a swing that must be made with a long iron. Also, the spectacular finishing hole on Retreat, reconfigured from a 460-yard par four to a pond-fronted par five by Rees Jones in 1998, reveals the ocean in the distance.

Later Joe Lee completed the 36-hole grouping with the Marshside nine, which weaves among the canals and tributaries of the property, occasionally unfurling sights of the ocean. It is highlighted by a pair of particularly perilous par threes, the third and seventh holes, which share the same water hazard.

Ultimately though, this remarkable assimilation of old-world ambiance, ocean vistas, luxurious amenities, and exquisite golf combines to make Sea Island a one-of-a-kind trip back through time.

Reynolds Plantation

GREENSBORO, GA

"Golf comes first
here and the beauty
speaks for itself."

Jack Nicklaus

"The traditions of Reynolds
Plantation are deep-rooted,
and the heritage of the land
and the beauty of the lake
are certain to leave lasting
impressions on
Great Waters golfers."

Mercer Reynolds

11th Hole-Great Waters
By Matt Scharlé

Swaying wildflowers in a white-fenced meadow along the entrance drive to the Great Waters Course at Reynolds Plantation beckon first-time visitors with a knowing assurance that what awaits beyond the incline of the next hill will be a treat for the senses and a golf experience not duplicated elsewhere in Georgia.

The twinge of anticipation that accompanies the eagerness to see what's in store sets the tone for the day on the Jack Nicklaus-designed, Lake Oconee-lined fairways. Built in 1992, Great Waters – which is the English translation for the Creek Indian word oconee – is the second jewel in the three-gem crown of championship courses at the Reynolds resort and residential community situated halfway between Atlanta and Augusta.

The Mercer Reynolds family of Greene County can trace its ownership of portions of the 6,000-acre former family plantation back to grants deeded by the King of England in 1773. The current generation began development of the amenity-laden resort community in 1985. It revolves around the three courses, which besides Great Waters include the original Bob Cupp-created Plantation Course opened in 1988, and the 1997-completed National Course by Tom Fazio.

But for all the merits of the overall development, and the complementing original and newest layouts, it is the Great Waters course that has solidified Reynolds Plantation's budding, world-class reputation. Host to the Andersen Consulting World Championship of Golf from 1995 to 1997, Great Waters has garnered so many "best new," "best of," and "overall best" awards from every significant national and in-state golf publication that the pro shop staff has stopped mounting them on the clubhouse walls.

But the most noteworthy item here is that for all its acclaim, in a very real sense the course is underrated. That's because all of the accolades focus, justifiably, on the drama created by nine separate lake-bordering holes. But little notice has been taken of the fact that the remainder of the layout, which weaves inland amid a maze of shortleaf pines, thick-trunked oaks, hickory, cherry, and dogwood is among Nicklaus' very best efforts. With gently rolling central Georgia terrain to work with, the renowned designer proved he has the capacity to allow the lay of the land to dictate the types of challenges the golfer will face, rather than delegating that to the impact of the bulldozer. Frequently criticized in his earlier work for requiring an aerial path as the exclusive option to any target, Nicklaus permitted the greens at Great Waters that are not fronted by water to accept a run-up approach. He even allowed the shape of the land to fashion three left-turning doglegs, the third, fifth and 12th holes, departing from his tendency to favor fade-friendly, right-turning holes.

Ultimately, the lasting impression is the final one, and the anticipation builds with each new revelation of Lake Oconee's surpassing charms. The devilish par four 11th, only 314 yards from the most commonly used blue tees, offers a full panorama of the lake off the hole's left side, the only west-facing view the jagged peninsula provides. Playing the hole requires precise execution of either a bold attempt at the green from an elevated tee, or a cautious plotting of two short shots. Either way, water is in play throughout, and odds are that upon retrieving one's ball from the cup, a player without a committed plan finds one or more ways to encounter the lake.

But this is just a building-block for what is yet to come. The signature 14th may be the second most photographed par three in Georgia, behind only Augusta National's 12th. It is comprised of two narrow peninsulas jutting from the mainland that are separated by a cove. If foamy whitecaps are dancing on the lake's green surface, a golfer might brace himself on the tee box's edge to inhale pine-scented breezes blowing over the water before returning to the task of guiding a golf ball to safety on the other side of the cove.

The finishing trio of holes are not only exceptional tests of skill and nerve, but they also offer a chance to linger over a captivating view eastward to an unspoiled forest in the distance. The 16th green and 17th and 18th tee boxes are aligned in a row along the outermost point of the peninsula, all affording the view while creating a problem for the golfer who should be concentrating on the formidable assignment of finishing the round.

But once the challenge of negotiating the well-conceived, risk-reward par five 18th is complete, and the time has come to depart, there's comfort in a last look at the fence-lined meadows, whose wildflowers now seem to be gently waving good-bye, while simultaneously beckoning you to return soon for another round.

Jackson House - Former Home
of the Reynolds Family
By Dick Botto

The Greenbrier
WHITE SULPHER SPRINGS, WV

What's in a name? Usually a name describes the object to which it refers. With that in mind, who would want to play golf on a course named for spiny bramble vines and bushes? Everyone would ... when the course is The Greenbrier in West Virginia. The name does not in any way describe this gracious golf resort, one that offers every imaginable amenity in the arsenal of Southern hospitality, despite being named for the Greenbrier Mountains in whose shadow the course resides.

The Greenbrier evolved from an area called White Sulphur Springs, which in the 1800s was home to a health spa and resort where the wealthy flocked to be among their own. A hotel was added in 1857, which although called the Grand Central Hotel gained the nickname "Old White." Nearby, on the estate of Russell Montague, the first full-fledged golf club in the United States, Oakhurst, was founded in 1884. Montague and visiting Scots held golf tournaments on the private links, and even awarded medals. Resort guests who watched the sport that had been imported from Scotland denounced it, claiming it was "insanity" rather than proper amusement for grown men.

The American public, however, disagreed, and golf quickly became the rage in the United States. In the early 1900's, the Greenbrier Hotel was built and gained instant popularity, in part due to the addition of a nine-hole golf

15th Hole
By Ray Ellis

course named the Lakeside. So popular was the golf that the course could not keep up with the demand. The 18-hole Old White Course, a tribute to the original hotel, was added, giving the resort its first championship course. Designed by Charles Blair MacDonald, an authoritative figure in early American golf history, Old White reflected typical Scottish flavor - severely sloped greens and deep bunkers along the fairways as well as the greens - and recreated some of the most famous holes from European links, such as the Redan at North Berwick, the Alps at Prestwick, and the Eden at St. Andrews.

A second 18-hole course, the Greenbrier, was built by MacDonald in 1924. Visiting the course as it neared completion, Walter Hagen declared it the most interesting resort layout he had ever seen. In 1977, Jack Nicklaus was commissioned to redesign the course in preparation for the International Ryder Cup Matches. Thanks to Nicklaus' skilled hand, the heavily wooded Greenbrier has become the most challenging of the three resort courses, featuring two- and three-tiered elevated greens closely guarded by deep bunkers.

The Lakeside also benefited from redesign when it was expanded to 18 holes in 1962. The design creation of Dick Wilson, the Lakeside is more demanding off the tee than its two counterparts, and features the longest hole at 579 yards, even though in total yards it plays the shortest.

The Greenbrier was the setting for an amusing anecdote in golf lore history In 1936, Alva Bradley, owner of the Cleveland Indians and guest at the resort, was hit on the backside by a golf ball as he prepared to putt. "How dare you drive from the fairway into an occupied green?!" shouted Bradley at his 23-year old assailant, who was quickly identified as a new Greenbrier employee. The young man was duly fired, but he insisted on his innocence because the offending drive had not originated on the fairway, but from a tee 335 yards away. After demonstrating his long hitting style in a round of golf with Bradley, the employee - Samuel Snead - was reinstated. Snead would be linked with Greenbrier for most of his career, returning as Golf Professional Emeritus in 1993.

Snead got his early golf experience with a club made out of a swamp maple with a knot on one end. One of his early drives, at age seven, lofted a stone through a church window. Snead's first job in the industry was as an assistant in a golf shop, and then in 1936 (the same year he hit Bradley in the pants), he placed third in the Cascades Open using a makeshift set of clubs. Greenbrier's golf manager offered him the chance to become a pro at White Sulphur Springs, and he was on his way to a legendary career that earned him many PGA honors, one of which still stands: he carded an 11 under par 59 in the 1959 Greenbrier Open, a record in sanctioned tournament play. He was the PGA golfer with the most wins from 1940 to 1963, and his fame along with Greenbrier's reputation for excellence made the resort a magnet for heads of state, captains of industry, and other leaders of society.

So long and stellar is the history of The Greenbrier that it well deserves its designation as a National Historic Landmark. It is a classic in American resort hospitality and a standard in the sport of presidents, as evidenced by the 29 (and counting) U.S. Presidents who have visited The Greenbrier. If one of the original five golfers from 1884 were to arrive on the scene today with gutta percha balls and homemade clubs, he would, no doubt, be astonished at how the sport and its facilities have matured. Astonished, and proud.

Spring Foursome
By Ray Ellis

Sugarloaf
CARRABASSETT, ME

It is a rare occasion when an artist has his breath taken away. That is exactly what happened when Ronal Parlin, who is recognized around the world for his awe-inspiring Maine landscapes, stepped onto the 11th tee at Sugarloaf Golf Club.

Located at the foot of Sugarloaf Mountain, the famed New England ski resort, this course was the brainchild of Peter Webber, who was, at that time, a local real estate developer. When he first envisioned a course on the present site, all he saw was a canvas of dense forest, thick underbrush, and large boulders. The Carrabassett River ran through the center, and wild bear, moose, and a large population of white-tailed deer roamed freely. Undeterred, Webber was committed to seeing his dream become a reality. Full support was given by Sugarloaf president Larry Warren, who wanted to make the ski resort a year-round facility. After a chance meeting with renowned golf architect Robert Trent Jones, Jr., Webber began to shape his vision.

The mountain, trees, and wildlife presented a unique challenge for Jones. To no one's surprise, he rose to the occasion, creating a spectacular golf setting which has

11th Hole
By Ronal Parlin

become the new standard for mountain golf. The design takes advantage of both the steepness of the valley and the pristine river that flows down the mountain. Jones threaded fairways through the trees, over brooks and streams, and along the natural flood plain. Dramatic elevation changes provide the golfer with magnificent views of the surrounding mountains and the valley below. Voted Best Golf Course in the state for 12 years running by "Golf Digest," it is a must-play for any golf enthusiast.

Accuracy and precision are rewarded more than brute strength. However, the difficulty of the challenge is softened by the alluring appeal of the setting, hence the course's nickname, "Beauty and the Beast." Particularly challenging are the first six holes on the back nine, which Jones calls the "String of Pearls." Each hole in the sequence winds along the edge of the Carrabassett River, with stunning backdrops provided by the 4,000-foot surrounding peaks. The clean mountain air, the sounds of rushing white water, and the all-encompassing beauty combine for an invigorating golf experience that is unparalleled.

Sports and nature lovers can take advantage of the many outdoor activities available at Sugarloaf, including fly fishing, white water rafting, mountain biking, tennis, and hikes through the woods. In the winter, Sugarloaf remains one of the premier destinations for alpine and cross country skiers.

Perhaps Jones described it best when he said, "Sugarloaf is certainly one of the most spectacular settings and courses that I've ever had anything to do with." Sugarloaf will surely take your breath away, just as it did Ronal Parlin's.

15th Hole
By Alex Kalinin

6th Hole - Bay Course
By Matt Scharlé

Seaview

GALLOWAY, NJ

Seaview
by Paul Lovett

The term "mecca" is not used very often in America when referring to a golf destination. But located across Reed's Bay from Atlantic City is just such a place. The Marriott Seaview Resort is a throwback to bygone years. Its elegant white four-story hotel, on 670 wooded acres along the southern New Jersey shoreline, has been the secret of presidents, celebrities, and CEO's for almost a century. Two very diverse golf courses, the Bay Course, a Donald Ross links course that winds along Reed's Bay, and the Pines Course, which is carved from the woodlands surrounding the hotel, are the shining stars of Seaview.

When Clarence Geist, an oil and gas magnate and avid golfer, became frustrated with the slow play at the Atlantic City Golf Course, his playing partner, Maurice Risley, was quoted as saying, "Mr. Geist, if I had as much money as you, I'd build my own golf course." With that, Geist told Risley, who was an Atlantic City realtor, to find him the land on which to do just that. Risley found the parcel just north of Absecon, and it was there that Seaview Country Club was built.

The man Geist hired to build his golf course was the legendary Donald Ross. Ross laid out the Bay Course in 1912, overlooking Atlantic City just across Reed's Bay. Seaview quickly became the nation's premier country club and was visited by many notables, including Warren G. Harding and Dwight D. Eisenhower. Harding said the two days in May of 1922 that he played at Seaview were the two greatest days he ever spent. No other club in the country had an indoor pool, a French chef, and chauffeurs who drove Rolls Royces and Pierce-Arrows. Every affluent club used Seaview as its standard.

Geist became known as eccentric and egocentric, well-known for using the phrase, "Do you know who I am?" Leo Fraser, one of the most imposing golf professionals in the game, and Seaview's pro in 1935, said, "It only cost a hundred dollars to join Seaview, but it took more than money to get in, and if Geist heard anyone complain about the price of anything, he'd just go up to them and say, 'Your resignation has been accepted.'" Fraser believed that for all of his idiosyncrasies, Geist had built the finest club around and was ahead of his time. There was nothing like Seaview in the rest of the country.

One need not have to be a golfer to enjoy staying at the Marriott Seaview Resort. A wide variety of amenities is offered to its guests: an award winning golf learning center, eight tennis courts, health club, walking and jogging trails, volleyball courts, meeting rooms, elegant dining room, and an indoor swimming pool.

Many tournaments have been played on Seaview's Bay Course, including the 1942 PGA Championship, won by Sam Snead. The Bay Course is also home to the LPGA Shop Rite Classic, whose past champions include Julie Inkster, Betsy King, and Annika Sorenstam.

Seaview has always been a special place. It has an aura all its own that will embrace you from the moment you turn into the drive and pull up under its portico. The smooth blending of turn of the century charm and modern conveniences makes Seaview a truly elegant bayside retreat.

5th Hole
By Don Patterson

Hershey

HERSHEY, PA

Sweet... a common word in golf, referring to the "sweet spot" of a club, or overheard in statements such as "Boy, that was a sweet shot." But the word "sweet" is nowhere more appropriate than at the Country Club of Hershey, where buckets full of Hershey Kisses always seem to be within arm's reach, and the locals can tell you the wind direction just by breathing in the chocolate-flavored air.

Milton Hershey dedicated his life to a vision. This vision was to create an entire community, built from nothing but a dream. Hershey's involvement with the candy industry began long before chocolate. It was with funds from the sale of his company Lancaster Caramel to the American Caramel Company of Philadelphia for $1 million in 1900 that he built the original Hershey chocolate factory, then proceeding to build a town around it, and continually developing new projects designed to enhance the quality of life in his community. Even during the Great Depression, the town of Hershey managed to thrive, due to a tremendous building campaign that took place during the 1930s, resulting in the construction of most of the town's major structures.

The Country Club of Hershey features two superior 18-hole golf courses, the East Course and the West Course, and is located just five minutes from the elegant Hershey

6th Hole - West Course
By Don Patterson

Hotel, which is listed on the National Register of Historical Places and has been the recipient of many hospitality awards. The legendary Ben Hogan was the head professional during the 1940s, when there was only one course; he would certainly be proud to see the award-winning golf complex today, which has been named a Silver Medal Golf Facility by "Golf Magazine."

Both the East Course and the West Course are laid on rolling hills, blanketed with over 175 varieties of trees. Mature oaks, pines, and maples rising from the lush Pennsylvania terrain lend distinction and character to the landscape. In the not-too-far-off distance, the twin smokestacks of the candy factory stand as proud beacons throughout every round.

The West Course, designed by Maurice McCarthy, opened in 1930. Traditional in its layout, it features more than 100 sand bunkers, only one water hazard, and average-sized bent grass greens, with only slight degrees of undulations. At 6860 yards, the par 73 West Course plays to a 131 slope rating from the back tees. The first hole has been selected as one of the best holes on the LPGA Tour and is the number one handicap hole on the course. An elevated tee high on a cliff is the spotlight of the 176 yard, par three, fifth hole, with Hershey's former house in the background. "Golf Digest" has ranked the West Course as one of America's 75 Best Resort Courses and consistently includes it in their top 100 list.

Renowned architect George Fazio was the mind behind the East Course masterpiece, which has hosted the LPGA Lady Keystone Open. Playing to a 7,061 yard par 73, the East Course greens are small, or medium-sized at best, with water coming into play on five holes. Fazio engineered grand, challenging finishes to both the front and back nines, with a 420 yard, par four ninth that plays to a heavily bunkered elevated green, and a 456 yard, par four 18th that is flanked by water on the left and a downhill second shot to another heavily bunkered green.

Guests of the Hershey Hotel and Hershey Lodge automatically receive playing privileges, and although it is not private, the Country Club of Hershey does offer memberships. The resort features numerous amenities and activities, including tennis, swimming, and large conference facilities, as well as an abundance of local attractions to enhance the entire experience.

To Milton Hershey, we say "thank you" for building a town centered around America's sweet tooth, and for the care that has resulted in such a phenomenal all-around experience.

8th Hole - Challenger
By Adriano Manocchia

Bay Hill
Orlando, FL

Bay Hill is Arnie's place. His name is synonymous with excellence, integrity, and character. All of these traits have been brought to his Lodge and Resort in Orlando.

The Bay Hill Club and Lodge harkens back to a time when private clubs offered comfortable on-site accommodations for its guests. This tradition is still very much a part of Bay Hill as Mr. Palmer sees that guests are as graciously looked after as club members would be.

The club was founded in 1961 by a group of Tennessee businessmen who invited Dick Wilson to bring golf to life in a picturesque orange grove. In 1965, Arnold Palmer played in a golf exhibition at Bay Hill with a young Jack Nicklaus. Palmer shot a 66 that day and fell in love with the course. He decided to make Bay Hill his winter home and, with a group of partners, purchased the club and lodge in 1970.

Arnie set out to redesign an already good layout and in doing so created one of the favorite and finest courses on the PGA Tour. The Bay Hill Invitational traditionally boasts the strongest international field of contestants apart from the Tournament Players Championship. This field assembles partly in tribute to a great layout and for the cause of supporting The Childrens Hospital, but mostly out of deference and respect for their primary peer and hero, Arnold Palmer. He is the "King," as many reverently refer to him, and the one to whom many of them owe their careers. Arnold Palmer created modern-day professional golf; furthermore, it is he who made the game so popular with the masses. Mr. Palmer's golf titles include four Masters, two

British opens, one U.S. Amateur, and the 1960 U.S. Open. He won over 80 tournaments worldwide and represented the United States seven times in the Ryder Cup Competition as either a player or captain. He has received virtually every award given out in the field of golf, and yet he remains the most accessible and humble figure in sportdom.

Arnold Palmer has done as much for charitable causes as anyone in the 20th century. His army grows as he gets older, and those who have learned or benefited from his generosity and example include small children, older retirees, and everyone in between.

Arnold and his wife Winnie have brought all of this spirit together into their management of the Bay Hill Resort and Lodge. Each of them plays an active role in the day-to-day operations of the place.

But for Arnie to be satisfied the courses must be good. Bay Hill has long been considered one of the best resort courses in America. Arnie's high standards will see that it remains that way.

The primary course is made up of the 3,600-yard Challenger course with the 3,500-yard Champion course. Another 3,100 yards comprises the Charger course.

The primary layout is long but fair. Water and sand guard every entry into the greens and demand well-placed iron play. The 18th hole has produced some of the greatest made-for-tv finishes in golf. In 1990, tour rookie Robert Gamez came to the 18th, trailing Larry Mize and Greg Norman. With one well-struck seven iron to a well-tucked

13th Hole - Champion
By Adriano Manocchia

pin, he made eagle and won the Nestle Invitational. Each year the hole is generally ranked as one of the toughest on tour. Past Bay Hill champions have been great players such as Payne Stewart, Nick Faldo, Andy Bean, Ernie Els, Fuzzy Zoeller, Tom Kite, Fred Couples, Phil Mickelson, Paul Azinger, Lorne Roberts, Gary Koch, and Dean Forsimer.

Bay Hill is the rare occasion one gets to play a most popular stop on the PGA Tour. The Lodge is comprised of 58 cozy rooms. When you stay you are a member of the club. You might see the Palmers at dinner or out riding bikes. The lodge caters expertly to businesses and families alike. Tennis courts, a swimming pool, and a fitness center all contribute to a well-rounded vacation.

When you visit, please say hello to Arnold and Winnie...and tfor all of us thank them for being such great ambassadors of the game.

18th Hole - The Ocean Course
By Gordon Wheeler

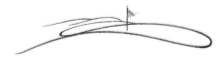

The Ocean Course
KIAWAH ISLAND, SC

17th Hole - The Ocean Course
By Graeme Baxter

It is highly doubtful that anyone ever thought of a sun-splashed island resort as an art gallery, but in one small way, at least one resort conjures up such a comparison. Kiawah Island, located just south of historic Charleston, South Carolina, is a resort community drenched in a virtual palette of vivid colors, rich in gorgeous ocean seascapes and panoramic landscapes. Here, golfers can sample the works of four masters of modern golf course architecture without leaving the island.

Pete Dye, Tom Fazio, Jack Nicklaus, and Gary Player have each fashioned a championship course from Kiawah's sandy dune ridges and subtropical canopies of pines, live oaks, and palmetto palms. The result is a collection of golf courses as diverse as the architects themselves.

The young but already world-renowned Ocean Course at Kiawah, where all 18 holes offer panoramic views of the Atlantic Ocean (ten of which play directly along the beach), earned almost instant acclaim as one of Pete Dye's best works shortly after it opened for play in May 1991. In less than four months, "Golf Magazine" ranked the Ocean Course among the 100 Greatest Courses in the World, making it the youngest course ever to make such a poll. "Golf Digest" named it the Toughest Resort Course and the third best overall resort course in the United States, behind only Pebble Beach and Pinehurst No. 2.

The Ocean Course at Kiawah will forever be remembered as the host of the 1991 Ryder Cup Matches and the site of the dramatic War by the Shore. This Ryder Cup battle went down to the last putt on the last hole of the last match on – you guessed it – the last day, with the United States posting a one-point victory.

This stunning course, formed from a ribbon of pristine sand dunes stretching nearly three miles along the Atlantic Ocean, is reminiscent of the great seaside links of England and Scotland. Dye took advantage of miles of oceanfront dunesland, bordered on one side by the rhythmic Atlantic surf and on the other by the-ever changing tidal marsh, and fashioned a course where every hole offers a view of the ocean.

Shapely contours of the land seem to have been manifested by the ever-present winds that sweep along the links. Dye created a variety of tees so that great holes would remain great holes, regardless of wind shifts, and so that players of all levels of ability could find a comfortable degree of challenge . "When the resort players see it, they'll be awestruck," Dye predicted. "They'll think it's the most difficult golf course in the world. But I think they'll find a very wide open type of golf course once they play it. I meant it to be that way. I was fortunate to have enough land to make it that way." The property is incomparable in the game of golf.

Another masterpiece on Kiawah is Osprey Point, a classic Tom Fazio layout blending artistry, challenge, and playability into designs that take maximum advantage of their natural setting. Ranked number 54 on the list of America's Top 75 Resort Courses by "Golf Digest," Osprey Point provided Fazio with a superb natural canvas on which to work his skill. The setting for the course, which was completed in 1986, features four large natural lakes, fingers of saltwater marsh, and dense maritime forests of century-old live oaks, pines, palmetto palms, and magnolias.

Jack Nicklaus' design, Turtle Point, has played host to numerous premier events, including the 1990 PGA Cup Matches, the club professionals' version of the Ryder Cup. Top players in the Carolinas Amateur, the Carolinas PGA, and the South Carolina Open have found Turtle Point to be a championship caliber test as well, where low profile fairways are blended into the existing landscape, and a keen eye and deft touch are required to master the gentle breaks of the greens. Opened in 1981, Turtle Point is a fixture in the "Golf Digest" list of the Best 75 Resort Courses, ranking 44th in the latest edition.

Opened in September 1996 Cougar Point Golf Course is the design accomplishment of Gary Player. Built on the site of the former Marsh Point Golf Course, Cougar Point follows the routing of its predecessor, but the new, par 72 layout retains little else from the original. All 18 green and tee complexes were redesigned and, in some cases, relocated. Every fairway was reshaped and lagoons were reconfigured, relocated, or even eliminated to accommodate the high handicapper, while providing a fair test for the scratch player. Water comes into play on 13 holes, and an abundance of sand underscores the premium that Cougar Point places on accuracy. The real personality of Cougar Point lies in its greens. Dramatic contouring within the putting surfaces makes precise iron play a prerequisite to good scoring.

As evidenced by the spectacular paintings by Gordon Wheeler and Graeme Baxter shown in these pages, time spent on Kiawah can be compared to time spent in one of America's finest art galleries. Both amateur and skilled players can appreciate the artistic environs of this glorious golf course.

14th Hole - The Ocean Course
By Gordon Wheeler

3rd Hole
By William Mangum

Pine Needles

SOUTHERN PINES, NC

Pine Needles Lodge and Golf Club shines as a beacon to old-world golf and modern-day comforts within the growing Sandhills area golf community of North Carolina. Let Peggy Kirk Bell, renowned worldwide for her golf teaching ability and pioneering contributions to women's golf, be your hostess at this relaxed and comfortable resort that is home to a 70-year old golf course designed by famed architect Donald Ross.

Today the Pine Needles Course remains vintage Ross, with most every tee, green, fairway contour, and obstacle existing as it did nearly seven decades ago, thanks to the ownership and management commitment of the Bell family. Both Pine Needles and its nearby companion course, Mid Pines, are considered fun to play. Narrow tree-lined fairways lead into small, quick bent grass greens. Both are shotmaker's courses that reward strategy and accuracy over brute strength.

When Ross built Pine Needles, golf carts did not exist, so naturally walkability was a consideration when laying out the course. Greens and the next tees were generally placed close together, unlike most modern courses that are stretched in order to provide more land on which to place real estate. Pine Needles was walker-friendly out of necessity when it was built, but remains so by choice today.

Golfers are offered the option of walking or riding, a trend currently growing throughout the sport.

"People in golf know about Pine Needles," United States Golf Association official Kendra Graham said at the 1996 U.S. Women's Open contested at the course. "It's a hidden gem." It is classic, old-style golf at its finest, the kind of golf that prompted Pat Bradley to remark at the same Open, "I've been playing Opens for almost 20 years now, and this is one of the better Open courses that I've ever played. It just flows from start to finish. And there are no gimmicks out there."

Pine Needles has also played host to the 1972 LPGA Titleholders Championship, the 1989 USGA Girl's Championship, and the 1991 USGA Women's Senior Amateur Championship, and it is slated to host another USGA Women's Open Championship in the year 2001.

In addition to coming to play an excellent course, golfers come to Pine Needles for an exceptional golf experience, including instruction through a variety of outstanding programs directed by Mrs. Bell and her son-in-law, former PGA Tour player Pat McGowan. "Our belief is that every good golf swing incorporates the same time-tested, rock-solid fundamentals," said Mrs. Bell, a charter member of the LPGA. "Each swing is different, but the basics are the same. Regardless of your level of ability or experience, we focus on creating a solid foundation and building from there." This philosophy coupled with her teaching ability, has earned Mrs. Bell the honor of being voted one of the six best women instructors in the United States.

Mrs. Bell's credentials within the golf community are without equal. She has won awards for her generosity in time and commitment to the game, including the USGA Bob Jones Award, the National Golf Foundation Joe Graffis Award, and the LPGA Rolex Ellen Griffin Award.

The cornerstone of the Pine Needles instruction program is the Ladies "Golfari," a phrase coined for its expedition-like qualities, where golfers have fun while seeking to improve their golf game. Guests arrive by

18th Hole
1996 U. S. Women's Open
By Kenneth Reed

lunchtime on the first day of their Golfari, then have five days interspersed with a careful mix of instruction and time to play golf or just relax. As McGowan noted, "A big objective is to make instruction fun. The game's tough enough as it is. We try to keep things as light as possible. Golfaris are as intense as you make them."

While the golf course certainly maintains its old world feel, it is kept in excellent shape, and has been completely regrassed, the bunker edges trimmed, and the sand replaced. Furthermore the resort is regularly privy to facelifts and upgraded amenities. Pine Needles offers golfers the best of both worlds ... the tradition of old-world grace and charm, blended in harmony with the contemporary comforts of the modern-day.

17th Hole
By George Lawrence

Bethpage
FARMINGDALE, NY

The word is simply ... intimidation. One might reasonably expect to suffer from it when the first sight seen on a golf course is a sign that reads "WARNING - THE BLACK COURSE IS AN EXTREMELY DIFFICULT COURSE WHICH WE RECOMMEND ONLY FOR HIGHLY SKILLED GOLFERS."

One might also suffer from intimidation standing on the 18th tee during the U.S. Open Championship holding a one shot lead.

These two gut-wrenching golf experiences may indeed coincide with the selection by the United States Golf Association of Bethpage State Park's Black Course as the host site of the 2002 U.S. Open. The selection of the Black Course marks the first time a public course has hosted the United States National Championship since WWII.

Located in Farmingdale, New York, Bethpage State Park features 90 holes of golf over five golf courses. The jewel of the five is the Black Course.

Widely accepted by golf experts as one of A.W. Tillinghast's finest works, the Black Course was completed in 1936 and was the last course designed by Tillinghast, master designer of such notable courses as Winged Foot, Baltursol, and Sunningdale. The Blue and the Red Courses at Bethpage are also Tillinghast's.

Ranked sixth in Top 100 Courses You Can Play in the United States by "Golf Magazine" and fourth in Top 75 Affordable Public Courses by "Golf Digest," the Black's reputation as a stern test of golf at 7,106 yards from the Blue Tees has been tested by many capable golfers. Multiple

tournaments, including the Metropolitan Open, USGA Junior Championship, and USGA Publinx Championship, as well as qualifying for the Senior PGA Tour Northville Long Island Classic, have taken place on the Black Course.

While always a difficult track, the Black Course wasn't always in the best condition. The 1960s and '70s saw the course deteriorate, almost to the point of no return. But when former athlete-turned-Governor Mario Cuomo took office, he set about restoring the facility to its former glory. Following a six-month reconstruction in the early '80s, the course was returned to its original pristine condition.

The Black Course, while recognized as tough, is also widely found to be a fair layout. The traditional traits of Tillinghast's work are evident. Bunkers generally border the fairways on only one side, while flanking either side of the putting greens. Greens are mounded and reveal pin

Bethpage Clubhouse
By George Lawrence

placements, but present tough recoveries from errant shots.

Doglegs define routing throughout the Black Course. The hardest hole, the par four fifth, plays to almost 450 yards. Players must carry bunkers at 225 yards from the tee and then navigate entry into an elevated green that is bordered by sand on the front, right, and rear. The course is generally open, but precision strategy is required coming into the greens.

As a 1,500-acre park on Long Island, Bethpage State Park is the destination for thousands of recreational visitors. None, however, are more enthusiastic on their departure than those who have taken on the Black Course and escaped unscathed.

15th Hole - Champions Course
By Dave Chapple

PGA National
PALM BEACH GARDENS, FL

PGA National. One of the most recognizable course names in golf, the mere mention of it bringing vivid images of picturesque Palm Beach scenery and the sport's most famous players to the forefront of every golfer's mind. Home of the Professional Golfers Association of America and the host site of the PGA Seniors Championship each spring, the resort boasts five championship golf courses and a golf academy, all located within minutes of South Florida's white sandy beaches, deep-sea fishing, world class polo, Worth Avenue shopping, arts complexes, and an abundance of fine restaurants.

It should not surprise anyone to learn that club professionals from around the country come to winter at PGA National, and many eventually retire to the year-round resort. True enthusiasts come to National because of the quality and diversity of the playing options that are available. Each of the five courses has held tournaments by virtue of its own individual merits, and each provides a unique experience for the players.

The first course, opened in 1980, was the Haig Course, named in homage to Walter Hagen. Designed by the uncle/nephew team of George and Tom Fazio, the gentle course offers a casual round for all levels of players. Hagen used to encourage friends to "stop and smell the roses" on the path of life, and as if to remind players of that wisdom, rose-bushes now bloom as 150-yard markers.

One year later, the Squire Course was dedicated by Gene Sarazen and immediately became known as a thinking man's course. The design duo of George and Tom Fazio cooperated on this course as well, and true to its namesake, the Squire demands accuracy off the tee and precise distance shots to its flags. The layout plays to 6,500 yards and features 63 bunkers and 17 water hazards. The par five, 506-yard fifth is a particularly challenging hole, where the golfer must successfully navigate water on the left and a deep sand-moated green at the finish.

The Champions Course was also opened in 1981, and it quickly gained acceptance as one of the toughest plays in the South. Originally designed by Fazio and Fazio, the course was redesigned by Jack Nicklaus in 1989-90 to accommodate more levels of players, while still offering enough of a challenge to satisfy the most respected tour players. Nerves are tested at every turn ... could it be due to the routing of the course, which brings water into play on 16 holes? Or perhaps it is the narrow landing areas that force the player to define a new strategy for each hole? The Par three 15th hole, starts the "Bear Trap," and has been featured on Nicklaus' ABC Special, The 18 Toughest Holes in Golf.' Strong winds blowing toward the water add another dimension to conquer, especially if the pin placement is on the far right, seemingly floating over the water.

The Champions Course has hosted some of golf's most prestigious tournaments, including the 1983 Ryder Cup matches and the 1987 PGA Championship. Nicklaus added gallery mounds for the thousands of patrons, fans and media who come for its annual events. The "Golfer" awarded the course inclusion in its Top 75 Resort Courses in the US and the Top 100 Golf Resorts in the World.

The General Course was named for and designed by Arnold Palmer, whose "armies" loyally followed him as he attacked courses and championships throughout his career. The course measures nearly 6,800 yards, with a feeling reminiscent of the Scottish links tradition. A St. Andrews-style double green comes into play as the eighth and 12th holes share the same putting surface. Undulating fairways wind through a maze of both grass and sand bunkers and water hazards. The greens are large and offer multiple entries to the hole. While the 18th is a scenic finishing hole with water threats on each shot, it is the 429-yard 17th hole that is the most challenging on the course. Be sure to negotiate your tee shot over the stream, and be prepared for a long second shot requiring pinpoint placement to the green flanked by bunkers on each side.

In 1988, PGA National purchased the Stonewall Golf Club and renamed it the Estate Course. The course is located approximately five miles from the resort and was acquired to accommodate the growing number of club professionals looking for on-site winter housing. It still serves as a primary site for the PGA Winter Tournament Programs, which attract over 1,000 contestants each year.

Swaying palm trees ... colorful waterlilies ... fascinating sea turtles ... varying degrees of difficulty from outstanding course to outstanding course. Is it any wonder that the mere mention of PGA National excites anyone who enjoys the sport of golf?

Turtle Sunbathing
By Dave Chapple

12th Hole
By Adriano Manocchia

"I knew I had walked into a painting as I looked across the pond at the 12th green. Distant hills disappeared in and out of the mist. The pine trees stood tall, enveloping the green. It didn't take long to realize the feeling I wanted to depict in the painting. My painting captures the course at 7a. m., splendid in all its southern mystique and charm."   *Artist Adriano Manocchia*

Duke University
DURHAM, NC

Duke University is steeped in rich history, and the aura permeating the campus is one of quiet strength. Recognized the world over for its outstanding sports program, it is not at all surprising that Duke University commissioned world-class golf course architect Robert Trent Jones to design its classic course in the North Carolina Piedmont.

The story of the design, construction, opening, and eventually the rebirth of the Duke University Golf Club is a tribute to the talents and persistence of many committed individuals. The origins of this gem date back to the early 1930s, when two Duke coaches, Wallace Wade and Eddie Cameron, began discussing the feasibility of carving the University's course out of the Duke Forest. A site was selected but was never actually formed due to the start of WWII.

It was not until 1955 that a new 120-acre site was selected for the elevation changes throughout its terrain. Sprinkled with meandering streams and blessed with a variety of hardwoods, towering pines, and beautiful shrubbery, the land was a pristine canvas on which to paint a classic course, and who better than Robert Trent Jones to bring the vision to reality?

University President Hollis Eden hit the first ball from the number one tee on September 26, 1957, to mark the opening of the Duke University Golf Club, which was immediately labeled as one of the top university golf facilities in the nation. Duke played host to the 1962 NCAA Golf Championships which, coincidentally, had among its field of players Rees Jones, the eldest son of course designer Robert Trent Jones. (The young Jones would follow in his father's footsteps, becoming a master architect in his own right.) With the hosting of this prestigious tournament, the Duke Golf Club had made its mark among the top university courses in the country.

To the dismay of many followers, the years were not

Duke Chapel
By Adriano Manocchia

kind to Duke's links, and the passage of time brought a serious decline in the quality of the once incomparable Duke layout. In 1988, Tom Butters, Duke University Vice President and Director of Athletes, recognized that while the routing of the golf course was magnificent, the condition of the course was not acceptable by Duke University standards, and therefore was in desperate need of restoration. Butters conceived a plan to fund the restoration of Duke Golf Club to its former reputation as "an outstanding golf course in superb condition." Approved by the Board of Trustees, the five-year plan was implemented.

And who better than the former NCAA player and son of the original course architect to complete the redesign plan? Rees Jones was clearly the only choice, not simply because of his associations with the course, but also because of his successful renovations of several U.S. Open sites, including Brookline, Hazeltine, Baltursol, and Congressional. Jones had set a new standard in modern golf course architecture with a style that he termed "definition in design." This style offers a significant level of clarity with holes that clearly indicate how they should be played, and it also utilizes the integration of the natural beauty of the land. Jones incorporates directional bunkering, visible hazards, and accessible target greens into his designs, further contributing to the playability of the course, a factor on which Jones places a premium both for present day and future play.

A perfectionist, Jones was a perfect match for Duke's high standards. He scrutinized every angle and considered every possible shot, insuring that every nuance of the course would be subtly engineered and perfectly placed.

Jones' success in achieving his goals at Duke is obvious for all to see. Duke Golf Club is quickly being recognized as a viable site for major tournaments and has been named the host course of the NCAA Men's Golf Championship in the year 2001. Duke has hosted the annual Duke Children's Classic, a proud tradition that has resulted in contributions of more than $8.5 million to Duke Children's Hospital, funds which have been used to support ground-breaking research and innovative medical treatments.

Lodging is available at the Washington Duke Inn, a landmark hotel that overlooks the course and houses the pro shop. This Four-Star, Four-Diamond award-winning hotel welcomes many players and visitors to its country inn atmosphere, and is as much a part of Duke's tradition as the course itself.

One cannot help but be in awe of Duke University's grand presence and be impressed by its commitment to excellence in education, as well as everything else associated with its name. The setting itself is all-at-once majestic, powerful, and serene. Golf artist Adriano Manocchia stated, "As I looked across the pond at the 12th hole, I knew I had walked into a painting. Distant hills disappeared in and out of the mist. The pine trees stood tall, enveloping the greens. It didn't take long to realize the feeling I wanted to depict in the painting. The painting would capture the course at 7 a. m., splendid in all its southern mystique and charm." Splendid, indeed.

Hartefeld National
AVONDALE, PA

Amid the rolling hills of Pennsylvania's Brandywine Valley outside Philadelphia, Hartefeld National exemplifies what a public golf facility can be. Cut through acres of mature trees and flowering plants, the immaculately groomed course and marvelous stone clubhouse rival the look and feel of the finest private country clubs. Grateful are we golfers to Davis Sezna, club owner, for making this state-of-the-art facility a public golf venue.

After years in the service and hospitality industry, Sezna had an excellent idea of what he needed to do to make this club unequalled. First, he recruited premier architect Tom Fazio to design the course. The property is wooded in some areas, and open in others, offering varying views from one hole to the next. The word most often used when first describing the course is "mature." True to his deserved reputation, Fazio was able to engineer a layout that appears as though neither a tree was moved nor a mound created. Hartefeld National was not designed to be notable in some distant future. On the contrary, it was outstanding on opening day.

Hardly a hole on the course is flat. Each one flows and plunges seamlessly over the contour of the land. Measuring 6,969 yards from the championship tees, the course plays to a 73.2 rating and 131 slope. To the relief of players of all

17th Hole
By Jesse Hyde

8th Hole
By Mike Ventola Sr.

levels, there are no blind shots on the course. Carts are not required, and many golfers opt to walk the gorgeous grounds, breathing in the beauty with each step.

The practice areas here are first class also. The practice putting green is spread over a full acre, and there is a full service golf school for players of all ages.

"Golf Digest" named Hartefeld National one of the Ten Best New Upscale Courses in the country in 1996, and "Golf Magazine" placed it in its Top Ten Public Courses in the nation almost immediately after its opening. Sezna always envisioned hosting championship tournaments, and in 1997, Hartefeld National was named the new home of the Senior PGA Tour's Bell Atlantic Classic.

Along with a magical course, Sezna knew he needed a special clubhouse. Situated on an historic family estate, the stone mansion heightens the "members only" feeling that

is found throughout the complex. Hardwood floors, oak-paneled walls, exposed beam ceilings, and six working fireplaces create a warm and inviting atmosphere of gracious hospitality. Relax in an Irish Pub, where antique clubs and black-and-white photos of golf legends such as Bobby Jones adorn the walls. Or take a stroll through a complete chronological history of the Walker Cup inscribed in gold leaf on the walls of the Walker Cup Room. Jay Sigel, whose Walker Cup Jacket is proudly displayed here, feels Hartefeld National is simply "unbelievable." Fittingly, Sigel was also the winner of the inaugural Bell Atlantic Classic held here. The Grille flaunts breathtaking views to accompany a good cigar after a satisfying round. Friendly staff and food that has been described as dazzling complete the picture, making Hartefeld both memorable and enjoyable.

Perhaps it is because Sezna happens to be one of Pennsylvania's top amateur golfers that he set out to create the ultimate golf experience. Whatever the reason, as anyone who has ever played Hartefeld National will attest, he accomplished just that. PGA Tour pro Mike Bodney said it best when he commented that "you just don't find public golf like this." Except here.

The Hartefeld National Clubhouse
By Jesse Hyde

18th Hole
By Linda Hartough

Harbour Town

HILTON HEAD, SC

Flags snap smartly to attention in the brisk sea breeze. Tartan-clad bagpipers parade past the shadow of a red-and-white striped lighthouse as top PGA tour players look on. Crowds of excited spectators gather alongside perfectly manicured emerald green fairways. A cannon is fired into the distance with a resounding boom, signaling the start of another MCI Classic - The Heritage of Golf, on the legendary Harbour Town Golf Links.

Located on the grounds of the world famous Sea Pines Resort on Hilton Head Island, Harbour Town Golf Links may owe its topography to the lush South Carolina low country, but its heart lies more than three thousand miles to the east, along the windswept coast of Scotland. There, world-renowned architect Pete Dye found the inspiration for the one-of-a-kind links-style course which he and his design consultant Jack Nicklaus sculpted from 300 acres of virgin oak and pine forests along the shores of Calibogue Sound. When designing Harbour Town, Dye was determined to bring forth the spirit of the past, which can be found at Scotland's fabled courses, for the benefit of a new generation of golfers. Instead of power, distance, and strength, Dye emphasized finesse. Replacing the wide open fairways and huge greens that were dominant in the late 1960s, Dye fashioned a tight, twisting layout with postage stamp greens and deep bunkers lined with railroad ties - an innovation that would soon become his signature. Quite simply, his creation would change the path of modern golf course design.

Today, Harbour Town Golf Links continues to delight and confound legions of amateur and professional golfers. Well-known as the home of The Heritage of Golf, it is one of the top stops on the PGA Tour. The colorful Old World pomp and pageantry of the opening parade give the Heritage a

distinctive personality, one which has captured the fancy of spectators and players since the beginning. Of course, Arnold Palmer's dramatic performance at the inaugural tournament did a lot to enhance the tournament's image from day one. His decisive win with a four-day score of 283 ended a 14-month dry spell, boosting his career and instantly cementing the tournament's reputation. The Winner's Circle at Harbour Town reads like a "who's who" of professional golf. Nearly every major player of the latter half of this century belongs to that list – from Arnold Palmer, Jack Nicklaus, Greg Norman, and Tom Watson, to Nick Faldo, Payne Stewart, Fuzzy Zoeller, three-time winner Hale Irwin, and remarkable four-time winner Davis Love, III. If, as they say, you can judge a golf course by its champions, then Harbour Town surely rates as one of the world's finest.

The rise of Harbour Town Golf Links and Sea Pines Resort paralleled the rise of Hilton Head Island itself. In the late 1960s - long before Hilton Head was a household name - Sea Pines founding father Charles Fraser and a handful of company executives decided that bringing a world-class PGA Tour event to Sea Pines would focus national attention on their fledgling resort. The brash new design of the course was as innovative as the resort itself, and was easily recognized as a worthy challenge for the game's greatest players. It seemed only natural that the name for the tournament should be derived from its historical Scottish connection and the game's time-honored traditions, hence the title "Heritage of Golf," first played in 1969.

Painstakingly sculpted from one of the most magnificent landscapes in golf, Harbour Town is a shotmaker's dream. It is a course that calls upon every resource a golfer can muster: pinpoint accuracy, unflagging concentration, and careful, strategic thinking, as well as every club in his bag. With its small, challenging greens, Harbour Town Golf Links is stunning proof of Dye's saying that "something that makes a golfer chip with finesse is a lot more interesting to him than a 95-foot putt." Nonetheless, the course is considered exceptionally well-balanced, with an interesting interplay of short and long holes. Harbour Town's par threes, in particular, have been lauded as one of the finest collections of par threes of any course in America. Also noteworthy is the scenic, albeit treacherous, 18th hole, a 478-yard par four, which plays alongside the breeze-swept shores of the Calibogue Sound.

The course itself is a study in architectural beauty. The signature finishing hole, bordered by the wide blue waters of Calibogue Sound on one side, trees on the other, and the famous candy-striped Harbour Town lighthouse straight ahead, is picture perfect for golfers and artists alike. Harbour Town was ranked in the top three American courses built since 1962 by the American Society of Golf Course Architects, and included in Top 30 Courses in the world by "Golf Magazine." "Golf Digest" consistently ranks it among its Top 100 Resort Courses, and it has often been cited as the number one course in South Carolina.

Perhaps the finest accolade given to Harbour Town was from "Sports Illustrated" magazine, which called the course "nothing short of a work of art." And who better to capture the essence of Harbour Town on canvas than golf artist extraordinaire, Linda Hartough, world-renowned for her awe-inspiring landscapes? All at once invigorating, innovative, exhilarating, gut-wrenching, and beautiful, the Harbour Town golf experience is exceptionally rewarding.

15th Hole
By Ray Ellis

World Woods

BROOKVILLE, FL

"Destination golf" is one phrase that aptly describes World Woods Golf Club, located 90 miles northwest of Orlando, Florida. "Golfer's paradise" and "golf at its best" are two more. This facility is something special, offering 36 holes of some of the best public golf in the United States, but most people have no idea where it is. Even the most stubborn driver who never stops to ask directions will find himself pulling into a gas station, frustrated. But frustration will give way to pure satisfaction when World Woods unfolds in front of you. The first impression for many golfers is , am I still in Florida? Rolling hills, heavily wooded with impressive pines and oaks, and perfectly manicured fairways, tees, and greens seem more like Pennsylvania than the typically marsh-like surroundings found in coastal Florida.

To its immediate credit, World Woods' two 18-hole courses are the design accomplishment of acclaimed golf course architect Tom Fazio. A genius in his trade, Fazio's method of design is to enhance the characteristics of the land by building upon its inherent qualities, resulting in a

15th Hole - Pine Barrens
By Paul Kuchno

course that appears to have been there all along. As Fazio himself states, "We allowed the land to tell us what to do." Each of World Woods' two courses is distinctly different in its design, due in large part to the landscapes upon which each was built.

The Pine Barrens, a 6,902-yard par 71, is a tight, intimidating layout named for its vast spreads of pine trees and barren waste areas. Tall straw-colored wild grasses border native sand bunkers, furnishing striking contrasts against the deep-green, well-maintained grasses on the fairways and greens. Fazio incorporated unconventional square and rectangular shaped tee boxes into the design, which provide yet another striking contrast to the conventional utilization of the natural landscape. Playing the Pine Barrens requires delicate placement after a long carry shot, prompting many to compare it to Pine Valley in New Jersey, generally considered to be the number one course in the world.

Rolling Oaks offers a traditional design for the serious golfer. The course's rolling hills are lined with a pristine forest of stately oak trees, their branches veiled in Spanish moss. Large, fast, multi-tiered greens, deep-blue water features, and cavernous bunkers filled with bright white sand challenge players amidst a beautiful array of colors. Springtime brings even more bountiful bursts of color, with an explosion of dogwoods, magnolias, azaleas, and other lush, flowering vegetation. Combine this setting with the closely manicured, wide-open fairways and expansive greens, and it is no wonder that many feel Rolling Oaks bears a close resemblance to Augusta National.

Players can prepare to face the challenges of the championship courses at World Woods on the number one ranked practice range in the United States. The massive 22-acre facility features eight separate teeing stallions, along with target greens and fairways, practice bunkers, and chipping and pitching greens. It is set in a round square form, giving golfers a chance to practice in various wind and sun conditions. One of the most memorable parts of this practice facility is the two-acre putting course, which features tremendous undulations, guaranteeing a challenge to even the best putters in the game. With 36 holes, it provides not only a great warm-up before a round, but great entertainment as well, and has been known to settle a bet or two after a match. There is even a nine-hole short course, featuring seven par three's and two par four's, making it a perfect place for juniors and beginners.

So remember: when you are positive that you must have gone too far, and that no golf course can possibly be worth this drive, keep going. It is well worth it. Once you step foot on World Woods, you will find yourself thinking at the end of the day, "If only the sun could stay out just a little longer...."

16th Hole - Pine Barrens
By Tom Lynch

15th Hole
By A. J. Rudisill

Blue Heron Pines

COLOGNE, NJ

Blue Heron Pines opened Memorial Day weekend 1993 and soon became the only four-star rated daily-fee golf course in southern New Jersey. "Golf Digest" gave the course this stellar rating in the 1998-99 edition of their popular guide, "Places to Play," and also the magazine named Blue Heron Pines one of the top three public courses in New Jersey in its January 1996 issue.

Designed by award-winning golf course architect Stephen Kay, who has designed and renovated more than 100 courses since 1977, the club and surrounding residential community are located just ten minutes from Atlantic City, 45 minutes from Philadelphia, and two hours from New York City. Carved out of the Pinelands of southern New Jersey on 325 pristine acres, the course is reminiscent of such classic courses as Pine Valley and Pinehurst No. 2. Kay has combined strategically placed bunkers, undulating greens, and glistening blue water ponds to create his visually striking masterpiece. While a few of the holes are of the "grip it and rip it" variety, most require patient course management and a thorough evaluation of the risks and rewards of playing a particular shot.

Set among ancient oaks and conifers, the club has paid special attention to the surrounding environment and is a member of the Audubon Sanctuary program. The area is a natural habitat for many species of wildlife, including egrets, purple martins, and the great blue herons after which the course is named.

Course owner Roger Hansen sums up the feelings of many with his observation that "Blue Heron Pines is a public golf course that has the distinctive look, feel, and atmosphere of a world-class private club." "Golfweek"

concurs: "In an era when golf's future lies with quality public courses, Blue Heron Pines sets the highest standards.... The course shows how far intelligence and imagination can go in making modern golf memorable."

The beauty continues in the impressive clubhouse, where the works of famed artist and sculptor Anthony J. Rudisill are on display, including his magnificent representation of the 15th hole and his masterpiece, "Blue Majesty." This exquisite life-sized sculpture of the great blue heron features individually carved and inserted flight feathers, and it took nearly three years to complete.

Like everything else at Blue Heron Pines, the golf shop is world-class. "Golf Shop Operations Magazine" recently named it one of the best 100 Golf Shops in America. It is the only daily-fee course in New Jersey to win this prestigious award that recognizes excellence in the golf retail merchandising industry. Just steps away from the shop is a massive 30,000 square-foot practice tee. Nearby are three practice putting and chipping greens. Blue Heron Pines is also home to one of the highly acclaimed Golf Digest Instructional Schools.

Blue Heron Pines has been rated as one of the top women-friendly facilities in North America by "Golf For Women" magazine. The listing includes public, private, semi-private, and resort courses in 36 states and Canada. "Blue Heron Pines is cited for its programs and policies that welcome women to golf and encourage them to stay with the sport," says Patricia Baldwin, the magazine's editor-in-chief.

While many clubs host tournaments that are combined with tennis, few can boast of a competition that combines golf with another event as singular as The

Ole Hansen & Sons Golf and Sporting Clays Invitational, which takes place at Blue Heron Pines. This novel event pairs golf with the fastest growing sport in the United States today, sporting clays, and gives new meaning to the term "Shotgun Start." Now 70 years old, Ole Hansen & Sons is a highly diversified privately held company based in Atlantic City, New Jersey. Its association with Blue Heron Pines has resulted in the tournament raising thousands of dollars for the local United Way charity.

Nestled among majestic pine trees with the sounds of native birds singing melodic background music, Blue Heron Pines offers the perfect serene setting for the golf enthusiast. And while seeming a world away, the glittering nightlife of Atlantic City is a mere "chip shot" away, providing a dramatic difference between day and night entertainment.

Blue Majesty
By A. J. Rudisill

Little River
CARTHAGE, NC

"Looking for the scene that has all of the elements that make up a great golf painting is more a gut feeling for me than anything else. I look for a scene that has an interesting foreground, a middle ground that features the golf scene, and a background that carries you far off into the distance. My gut told me that this scene, of all the beautiful ones at Little River, really summed up the property perfectly."

Artist Matt Scharlé

8th Hole
By Matt Scharlé

Little River is the newest addition to an already impressive list of golf courses in the North Carolina Sandhills. But what sets it apart from the others are the topical differences of the terrain, which makes Little River seem more like a combination of the Piedmont foothills and the plains of the Midwest, than the Sandhills, which are characterized by sandy soil and pine trees.

Located just five miles north of the infamous traffic circle in Pinehurst, the Little River Golf Club is the product of noted architect Dan Maples. Situated at the southernmost tip of the Uwharrie Mountains, an ancient range worn down to little more than hills now, sits a narrow belt of land where the Uwharries blend into the Sandhills. It is this belt that forms the diverse canvas for Little River. "Although it's in the Sandhills, it's kind of on the edge," stated Maples. He carved the course from 700 acres of rolling clay hills with nearly 200-foot elevation changes, broad basins bisected by narrow rivers and streams, and thick forests of both hardwoods and pines. While the setting belies its Sandhills location, the quality of the course has earned Little River a superior reputation among the more than 40 courses that comprise this area, widely recognized as one of golf's premier destinations.

Maples has said that while much of the front nine reminds him of a prairie, the course offers so many different views, that seeing just one area does not do it justice. "Just because you've seen one area doesn't mean you've seen what the golf course looks like," says the architect. An outstanding example of this course's diversity can be seen on the first and fifth holes. The first features a promontory-like tee overlooking a scenic lake. Sweeping elevation changes and massive oaks characterize the first four holes, but at the fifth the hills and oaks are replaced by a park-like setting formed from low lying pasture land. The gentle contours and intervening wetlands provide the backdrop for the rest of the front nine.

After the turn, Little River continues to demonstrate its chameleon-like personality, changing to fit the scenery. On the back nine, the land has quite a different look, with tall poplar, gum, and sycamore trees adding to the mountainous feel of the area. Immediately introducing a challenge, the par-four tenth hole is situated on high open land, which then plunges all the way down to the banks of the river by the time you reach the 13th green. After playing along the river for four holes, with nearby sycamore, poplar, and gum trees reaching high in the air, the course climbs back up onto solid ground, reaching its pinnacle on the tee at the 17th. From this, the highest point on the course, the player can see for miles, although the green is not in his field of vision, thanks to a slight dogleg right, 140 feet below the tee.

Owners Bobby and Barbara Blanche take pride in the preservation of a variety of structures from the original farm that occupied the land. Once a dairy farm, the site became a horse farm and included race tracks and show arenas. Some of the old buildings come into play throughout the course, such as the one-horse holding sheds on the ninth green. The 18th plays directly into the circa 1890 barn that is now home to the clubhouse, which is a wonderful place to relax and unwind in a comfortable atmosphere.

The Little River Golf Club is certainly worthy of its location. Retired "New York Times" golf writer Gordon White says, "Little River is Dan Maples' best piece of design." There may not be another course, either in this area rich with magnificent golf or anywhere else, that looks or plays like Little River.

Clockers Tower
By Matt Scharlé

16th Hole - The Legends
By A. J. Rudisill

Chateau Elan

BRASELTON, GA

Nestled in the north Georgia countryside is a gorgeous gem known as Chateau Elan, built in the style of 16th century France. Rising from rolling hills blanketed in a carpet of lush green grass, this treasure is a feast for all the senses.

As you drive through the resort's gates, you are greeted by a visual array of beauty. One's eye travels first to the unexpected trellises of grape vines, then continues up an incline to the Equestrian Show Center and the handsome stallions grazing about. On summer evenings, beautiful sounds float from the outdoor concerts performed at the open air Center. Of course, the Chateau itself, constructed from fieldstone, commands great respect and admiration for its elegance and tradition. Three 18-hole courses, a beautiful nine-hole par three walking course, a world-class Stan Smith-designed tennis complex, and a European health spa complete the picture.

Responsible for this unexpected delight is Donald Panoz, an Irish businessman with an uncanny ability to see opportunity where others see obstacles. A true visionary, Panoz is a man who sees his ideas come to fruition through dedication and determination. Chateau Elan began as a winery when few people believed grapes could grow in the humid climate of Georgia. "I've found that when there are things that make sense and are still challenging, it's very rewarding to do them," says Panoz. Although Panoz knew from the outset that the winery would be only a small part of his larger vision, his commitment to excellence prevailed, and he built a winery that produces 500,000 bottles each year, with wines that have won more than 250 awards.

Further evidence of his ambition to overcome a challenge came when Panoz envisioned bringing together three legends of golf to create a tribute to the golf course architecture of the early 1900s. Amazingly, he did just that. The Legends at Chateau Elan is the masterpiece of celebrated golf greats Gene Sarazen, Sam Snead, and Kathy Whitworth. Each selected six of their favorite holes to emulate, and The Legends course was born. Golf enthusiasts will be excited to find such recognizable holes as the 12th and 13th at Augusta National; the Postage Stamp at Royal Troon; and the 18th at Merion, the setting for Ben Hogan's renowned one iron approach in the final round of the 1950 U.S. Open. Art and golf enthusiasts alike will appreciate the statues of the three legendary players which grace the clubhouse lawn, as well as the Gene Sarazen Museum located in a cottage on the resort's property.

This member and resort guest-only course is home to The Subaru Sarazen World Open Championship, an annual tournament which debuted in the fall of 1994. Also called "A Gathering of Champions," the Sarazen invites the winners of all of the world's Open Championships to compete for the Double Eagle Trophy.

The Legends was actually the second course conceived at Chateau Elan. The first 18 holes were carved out of 170 acres of the property's finest terrain, creating The Chateau Course, which was instantly recognized as one of the top courses in Georgia. Designed by Denis Griffiths, the course winds along three lakes and two creeks. Understandably, water comes into play on ten of the 18 holes, while 87 bunkers lend challenge and character to the lush fairways and bent grass greens contained in its 7,030 yards.

The Woodlands course, also designed by Griffiths, opened in 1996. Many consider it to be the most picturesque of the three championship layouts. Numerous *elevations present memorable views, and each hole is tree-lined, giving players a feeling of serenity and solitude.*

Another small gem in this treasure known as Chateau Elan is the popular nine-hole par three course. While short in length, the layout of the course still provides a stimulating challenge amidst breathtaking beauty, making it the perfect choice when time does not allow a full round of golf.

The practice facility at Chateau Elan is home to the *southeast regional Golf Digest Instructional School, and has been rated the number one practice and teaching facility in the state. Of particular interest is a "Wee Links" three-hole short game course, focussing on putting, chipping, pitching, and bunker play.*

Chateau Elan is rare in its beauty. Rarer still is the dream and determination of a man who makes things happen. Donald Panoz is such a man, and all who visit Chateau Elan have the privilege of enjoying his vision.

Legends Clubhouse
By A. J. Rudisill

2nd Hole - The Woodlands at Chateau Elan
By Matt Scharlé

16th Hole
By Adriano Manocchia

"When I first walked the course, it was 5 a.m., a typical Florida rain shower had just passed. It was pure magic. Contrary to what had been suggested (the famed 17th Island Hole), I stopped behind the hole on the 16th. The wooden bulkhead, clouds, birds, and rolling greens were all there waiting to be captured on canvas." *Artist Adriano Manocchia*

TPC Sawgrass
JACKSONVILLE, FL

As varied as the colors of a crimson-stained sunrise on the coast of northern Florida are the wide range of opinions about Pete Dye's trademark island greens and railroad-tie reinforced bunkers. Love them or hate them, there's no denying he got them right when designing TPC at Sawgrass Stadium Course in Jacksonville, Florida. And he did it in a most spectacular natural setting.

Host site of The Players Championship, the Stadium Course is the birthplace of grass mounding, otherwise known as "natural bleachers" for tournament spectators. At the Stadium you can sit and watch the likes of Woods, Norman, Price, Love, and Couples without the aid of even a stool. But sitting is somewhat unlikely as the drama of the event unfolds.

Number 17 of the Stadium Course, the famous par-three island hole, plays a pivotal role in every tournament. At a maximum of 132 yards, swirling winds and imposing water create navigational concerns and strong psychological distractions. Tournament outcome often rests on a player's performance here.

Treachery waits throughout the 6,857-yard course. Expect massive sand waste areas, lakes, and ponds, and Scottish link-style bunkers. Deliciously speedy greens are the final hurdle to overcome.

Another expectation of TPC at Sawgrass is accolades, and the Stadium Course does not disappoint, including the ranking of seventh in America's Best Resort Courses and fourth in difficulty by "Golf Digest." And "Southern Links" calls the split fairway 11th hole one of the Best Par 5's in the South.

While visiting TPC at Sawgrass, you'll want to make time for the many other courses and activities in the Jacksonville area. The 4,800-acre Marriott at Sawgrass Resort is the second largest golf resort in the United States and the Official Hotel of TPC at Sawgrass. Of the four other on-site courses, a tough complement to the Stadium Course is TPC at Sawgrass Valley, crafted by Pete Dye and Jerry Pate. Water often comes into play on these 6,838 yards. Fairways filled with hills and valleys create additional challenges. Uncharacteristic of an abstract Dye course, few roughs exist so there are fewer interruptions of executable shots. The Oakbridge Course boasts a beautiful setting, where natural wildlife, water oaks, and Spanish moss can be found in abundance.

At Sawgrass, home of the PGA Tour, golf is a way of life – a way of life served up in a mix of savage and sophisticated play that is pleasurable for both the proficient golfer and the weekend duffer.

17th Hole
By Ray Ellis

9th & 18th Hole
By Diane Selby

Osprey Cove
ST. MARYS, GA

The first golf course in Georgia one finds when travelling north on I-95 out of Florida makes a distinctive statement of transition between the golf settings to be found in these neighboring states. At Osprey Cove Golf Club in St. Marys, a lush pineland forest at the edge of a river basin contrasts with the palm-lined fairways of its southern neighbor. And what's more, those arching Georgia pines at Osprey Cove impressively depict just what the dominant environs of the golf experience are throughout the state.

But even more than alerting the traveller of a shift in the landscape, Osprey's 930-acre planned development, which includes 475 homesites, was a key factor in this coastal town's 1997 designation by "Money" magazine as the number one small town in America.

Just off Georgia's first exit on the interstate the property sits on land that was once another golf course, a nine-hole public facility built by the town's leading corporate citizen, Gilman Paper Co. In 1990, Gilman plowed the course under and turned it over to PGA Tour professional Mark McCumber to create the championship, 18-hole layout that has acquired a distincitve links-land flavor as it has matured. Snugly set beside the vast salt marshes of the mammoth St. Marys River basin, five of Osprey's holes provide vistas of the wetland that set's this golf course apart from the norm and that has earned it considerable national acclaim.

The marsh first comes into view on the 423-yard, par four eighth hole, ranked the course's most difficult. It bears a striking resemblance to the fabled 18th at Hilton Head's Harbour Town Course, minus the lighthouse. A huge bulge of a landing area for the drive extends left toward the marsh

15th Hole
By Diane Selby

and creates the similar look and shot value between the two holes. From the vantage point of that bulge in the middle of the fairway, a long look to the left across the marshland reveals a white-walled cliff in the distance, which besides affording a dramatic backdrop of the river basin, also happens to be in Florida.

The par four ninth continues along the same path, with the marsh skirting its left border, and culminates a huge double green it shares with the par five 18th. This is the signature stamp most commonly associated with the course, and the clearest expression of McCumber's links-land intent.

Approaching from the opposite direction, the par four 15th, the par three 17th, and the finishing 18th are bordered to the right by the marsh and are the strongest holes on the backside. They offer a wonderful diversity of shot value, climaxing with a forced carry from the 18th tee box over a sea of swampy reeds that is a frightful undertaking when the wind is whipping.

Indeed, the course is designed, like most links layouts, with the wind in mind to act as the primary defense mechanism. When it is gusting, the five-hole stretch of marsh-bordering holes are well-managed by bogey golf, while the rest of the course is converted to the low-ball hitting, links-sytle layout that McCumber envisioned.

Typical of venues proximate to the ocean, Osprey Cove is rich in plant and wildlife. Just to the north is the 500,000-acre Okefenokee National Forest, with which Osprey shares a multitude of plant and tree species, including its fairway-skirting palmettos. In addition to its namesake ospreys and coveys of egrets and herons, one of the most unusual animals that makes Osprey Cove its habitat is the fox squirrel. This starkly colored, black and white mammal has unfettered roaming rights over the acreage, and is an amusing curiosity for its frantic, four-legged gallop across fairways as it tries to elude the approaching golfers.

St. Marys can also attribute its "Money" magazine recognition to both a high-tech job market associated with the King's Bay Naval Base, home of the Trident Nuclear Submarine, and the quaint ambiance of an antebellum fishing village. Having avoided the path of Sherman's march to the sea, numerous Civil War-era homes still stand and have been converted to bed and breakfast inns, shops, restaurants, and museums along oak-shaded Osborne Street, which runs through the center of town. Neighboring Cumberland Island, once the winter vacation spot of the Andrew Carnegie family, is the southernmost barrier island in Georgia, and, consistent with the area's timeless charm, is accessible only by ferry.

It all acts as an irresistible lure for people seeking the combination of small town Southern hospitality, a natural seaside setting, and a modern residential community with first-rate golf to call home – as the ospreys also do.

13th Hole - The Copperhead Course
By Adriano Manocchia

Innisbrook
TARPON SPRINGS, FL

Just south of the Greek sponge-diving community of Tarpon Springs, Florida, and minutes from the Gulf of Mexico, is the Westin Innisbrook Resort. One of America's premier golf and conference destinations, Innisbrook is situated on 1,000 acres of rolling hills in Pinellas County. With 72 exhilarating holes of golf set among natural lakes, woodlands, and hilly terrain, it is a wonder for any golf enthusiast to behold. The fairways are immaculate, the greens are fast, and the designs are diverse. Is it any wonder that all of Innisbrook's courses have consistently been ranked among the country's best?

Copperhead, a 7,087-yard par 71 course, has been rated the finest in Florida, and "Golf Digest" magazine has ranked it among the Top 50 Resort Courses in the country. It is the home of the JC Penney Classic, a unique year-end tournament that teams up the best players from the PGA and the LPGA Tours. With an outstanding field of players, the JC Penney attracts more than 100,000 spectators each year. The tournament returns 100% of all ticket sales to Tampa Bay charities, consistently contributing over $700,000 annually.

Also ranked among the country's Top 50 Resort courses is the challenging Island Course. Voted Florida's Most Interesting Course by a panel of golf professionals and writers, the par 72 Island Course measures nearly 7,000 yards from the championship tees.

Two brand new 18-hole courses have emerged from what was originally the Sandpiper Course. Hawk's Run is now the shortest of the resort's four courses, measuring 6,260 yards. Eagle's Watch was constructed from a combination of nine new holes and the front nine of the former Sandpiper. Wide fairways, steep hills, and sparse trees nurture the feeling of playing on Scottish links. The ever-present breezes blowing off the Gulf of Mexico only add to that feeling.

Innisbrook also offers a series of instructional programs for both beginners and advanced players. Sessions are offered throughout the year, with the addition of a special Junior Golf program that is available in the summer months.

The entire resort at Innisbrook is a study in excellence and quality. "Good Enough" is not a saying that is accepted by the staff. Guest accommodations are luxurious suites in villas named after some of the world's greatest golf courses. Three clubhouses grace the grounds, containing a variety of restaurants and lounges designed to satisfy a variety of taste preferences. The Tennis and Fitness Center offers 11 clay and two Laykold courts, along with three indoor racquetball courts. Full spa facilities serve to pamper and refresh with a generous array of treatments.

At the heart of the resort is the Innisbrook Village, a centerpiece that houses the reception area, specialty shops, restaurants, and pro shop. Recognized for its commitment to being a family resort, Innisbrook offers a plethora of activities for families to enjoy. Located only a short distance from Busch Gardens, the Florida Aquarium, dog and horse racing, the Salvador Dali Museum, Walt Disney World, beaches, and deep sea fishing, Innisbrook features more than meets the eye.

Cypresses, azaleas, hibiscus, citrus groves, and towering pines draped with Spanish moss provide bountiful bursts of color and aroma that will awaken the senses. After an invigorating day of golf, a quiet stroll along the grounds of Innisbrook completes an already perfect day.

By Adriano Manocchia

Wintergreen
WINTERGREEN, VA

The majestic presence of the Blue Ridge Mountains in the distance...the legendary Shenandoah Valley and Appalachian Trail merely steps away...an abundance of colorful mountain wildflowers shaded by a grand umbrella of oak and hickory trees: these are but a few of the natural riches to behold at the beautiful Wintergreen Resort in Virginia. Few resorts have the power to satisfy mind, body, and spirit more thoroughly than Wintergreen.

Planted firmly among some of the oldest geological formations in North America, the resort dances among the clouds at an elevation of 3,850 feet. Wintergreen beckons to golfers who are in the sport for the love of the outdoors as much as for the challenge of the game. Wintergreen delivers in both departments, with 45 holes of championship golf carefully designed to showcase the indigenous landscape, while protecting its vegetation. Two courses were molded from 11,000 acres of mountain landscape, with a 6,000-acre area dedicated as permanent, undisturbed forest land filled with hiking and riding trails, lakes, and streams. It is no wonder that the resort is highly

16th Hole - Stoney Creek
By W. D. Wood

regarded and considered one of the most sought-after recreation destinations in the country.

Wintergreen's two courses, often referred to as "Dr. Jekyll and Mr. Hyde," offer very different golf experiences. The storied Devil's Knob was Wintergreen's first course. Opened in 1977, it boasts the highest elevation of any course in Virginia. Golf architect Ellis Maples was mindful of the awesome 50-mile views of the Blue Ridge Mountains, and used them to great advantage in his design. He masterfully crafted the course to rest on the crest of mountain summits and wind its way through hardwood forests, rock outcroppings, brooks, and ponds. While much of the course is surprisingly level, Devil's Knob serves up plenty of challenge. Long drops of up to 250 feet over undulating fairways and well-clipped, protected greens provide significant degrees of difficulty. No wonder the course is rated among the best in the state.

Snow prohibits year-round play in this higher elevation, so golfers have to be content to enjoy this course during the warmer months. Spring begins the golf season here, bringing with it bursts of colorful florals, such as rhododendrons, mountain laurel, azalea, dogwoods, and wildflowers. Cool mountain breezes ensure comfortable play even in the hottest summer months. In the fall, a stunning palette of warm autumn colors welcomes all who visit. The rich sienna, bronze, orange, and yellow contrast sharply with the dark green pines, creating a memorable visual display.

Distinctly different from the high reaches of the Devil's Knob course are the more temperate holes of the Stoney Creek course, designed by Rees Jones. Stoney Creek is rated 34th in the nation among resort courses, and second in Virginia by "Golf Digest." The golden cornfields, pastures, farmland, and rolling hills of Stoney Creek are in such sharp contrast to the mountain setting of Devil's Knob, that it has been compared to playing in distinctly different parts of the country. The course lies in the Rockfish Valley, beside Lake Monocan. Designed in the late 1980s, Stoney Creek's original 18 holes were expanded to include the acclaimed Tuckahoe Nine. Together they fulfill Jones' vision for golf at Wintergreen. The two blend seamlessly, offering 27 holes that challenge and delight golfers as they turn each surprising corner. Never allowing a dull moment, the course ripples over hills, through woods, and across meadows, meandering past preserved wetlands and into plentiful water hazards, mounds, and bunkers, producing a thoroughly invigorating round of golf.

In keeping with Wintergreen's dedication to preservation of the natural environment, both courses have been thoughtfully sculpted into the natural terrain to complement it, not reconstruct it. Rather than imposing their design on the mountain the architects scrupulously allowed the mountain to dictate the course layout. The area referred to as a "botanist's paradise" was left untouched. Towering mature trees rise from a ground that is blanketed with wildflowers and native shrubs, resulting in a feast for the senses. Wintergreen has successfully tried to protect the careful balance between development and preservation, and in the process it has become an attractive destination, as the demand for its facilities proves.

9th Hole - Devils Knob
By W. D. Wood

15th Hole
By Alex Kalinin

Callaway Gardens
PINE MOUNTAIN, GA

Befitting the vision of its founders who avowed that nature could be enhanced for the benefit and enjoyment of all, the 63 holes of championship and resort golf at Georgia's Callaway Gardens are among the most immaculately groomed and visually appealing to be found anywhere in the country.

So much so, in fact, that the PGA Tour's best kept secret, The Buick Challenge, which has been contested on Callaway's Mountain View course since 1991, consistently ranks among the top five choices of Tour players for best conditioned course of the year.

The vision that drove the creation of Callaway Gardens belonged to Cason and Virginia Callaway, who opened the 14,000-acre nature retreat and resort in 1952. Situated 80 miles southwest of Atlanta, it occupies the eastern slope of Pine Mountain, the southernmost ridge of the Appalachian mountain range.

Callaway, a native of neighboring mill town LaGrange, first acquired 2,500 acres in the hilly region to serve as a laboratory for farming experiments. Over the years, his land acquisitions grew to 40,000 acres while his wife Virginia's keen interest in the region's natural beauty grew in equal proportions. A significant discovery she made on the property was the plumleaf azalea, a rare, late summer blooming flower that serves as the Gardens logo.

Among the attractions that Virginia nurtured into existence at Callaway are the Cecil B. Day Butterfly Center, a five-acre horticultural center, a seven-acre vegetable garden, and over 25 miles of walking, biking, and driving trails.

Not to be overlooked in the midst of this carefully tended habitat for nature is the golf experience. From the outset, Cason recognized that a well-maintained golf course was a logical extension of his and Virginia's philosophy for the Gardens' development. Consequently, he exerted a strong influence over designer J.B. McGovern's routing of the original nine holes of the Lakeview course to take full scenic advantage of spacious Mountain Creek Lake. It opened for play along with the Gardens in 1952, and proved to be a popular attraction immediately.

Ten years later, Dick Wilson added nine woodland holes, thus completing the first 18-hole championship layout. Wilson and his long time associate Joe Lee then constructed the Mountain View Course in 1965. They added Garden View in 1969, and an executive nine-hole layout, Skyview, rounds out the 63-hole complex.

It is the Mountain View course, though, with its PGA Tour pedigree, that is the primary golf attraction for first-time visitors. And it is this course which may be recognized one day as historically significant for a design style that bridged the gap between the pre-World War II "golden era of architecture" and the modern-day period, with its emphasis on physical features that create a striking visual impression.

Wilson and Lee embraced the simplicity of the golden era, yet used to full effect the technology and equipment at their disposal to craft dramatic design elements from difficult landscapes. Nowhere is this dual feat better demonstrated than at Mountain View. Its entire front side, along with the tenth hole and the two closing holes, is routed along the gentle rolls at the base of the mountainside. Here, the Wilson-Lee classicism is at work with the presentation of straightforward, pure golf that winds through thick pine forest and that is reminiscent of old northeastern courses like Winged Foot and Westchester. Elevated greens with strategically protective bunkering complete the likeness.

But then, the bulk of the back side climbs steadily up the eastern face of the mountain ridge, thereby affording long range vistas of tree-top horizons, and climaxing on a steep slope on which the parallel par four 14th and signature par five 15th holes are located. At the bottom of the slope sits Upper Falls Lake, which provides the right side border for the entire 15th, as well as the left side hazard of the par three 12th across the way.

It is this group of holes from 11 through 16 that

provides the spice at Mountain View with their elevation and lake-influenced decision making. But the real artfulness of Wilson's and Lee's design lies in the seamless manner in which the transition is accomplished. The player will hardly notice his ascent up the mountainside until he knocks one over the green at the 14th and finds himself playing back up a huge hill that is usually difficult to negotiate in just one swing.

Further down the slippery slope, the 520-yard 15th is among the most harrowing water-guarded challenges a golfer is likely to face anywhere. With the fairway tilting to the lake all along its length, the visually serene complement to its surroundings is transformed into a stress inducing ball magnet.

But whether it's a PGA pro trying to nail down victory on Sunday who is passing through the 15th, or the recreational player accepting that same challenge, one's success on the golf course is usually eclipsed by the memory of Callaway Gardens as a testament to the timeless beauty of nature carefully looked after by man.

The Hermitage
NASHVILLE, TN

Country music and the Grand Ole Opry are certainly the first things that come to mind in any discussion of the attractions found in Nashville, Tennessee. But the country music capital of the world is also quietly building a reputation for quality golf courses that are available for public play.

Foremost among the list of challenging, playable layouts is the Hermitage golf course, located seven miles east of Nashville's glitter along the gently flowing banks of the Cumberland River. The Hermitage is named for the stately residence of former President Andrew Jackson, which is preserved nearby. Measuring 6,775 from the back tees, the course plays to a slope of 122 and a USGA rating of 71.9. First time players can't help but be impressed by the manicured fairways and pristine, well-groomed greens throughout the layout. The condition of the course is taken seriously here and is kept in near-perfect condition all year long.

The Hermitage was designed by Gary Roger Baird and opened for play in 1985. Built primarily on the flat terrain inherent to the Nashville area, the course manages to present some challenging lies that are the result of Baird's innovative mounding. Though the flat topography would usually dictate a links-style course design, Baird opted instead for a more traditional look and feel. Water hazards,

11th Hole
By Paul Kuchno

drawn from the eight ponds and a lake on the property, are present on 16 of the holes, and 76 sand bunkers dot the fairways and border the greens.

Depicted here in Paul Kuchno's fabulous watercolor is the monster par five, 11th hole. The number one handicap hole on the course, it measures a whopping 600 yards from the back tees; no one has ever reached the green in two. Tee shots must contend with out-of-bounds to the left, trees and water to the right, and a follow-up approach shot over water to an elevated green. This hole is certain to make nearly everyone's "most memorable" lists.

The Hermitage is one of two courses presently owned and managed by Danner-Eller Golf Properties. The other, Willow Creek, is located in Greenville, South Carolina. The company reflects the successful union of the experience and management expertise of the two principals, Ray Danner and Mike Eller, who both love the sport. A philosophy of seamless service impeccably delivered in a relaxed, sporting atmosphere is the hallmark of this company that hosts more than 100 corporate, executive, and charity golf events each year. It is no wonder that the Danner-Eller golf properties have been lauded as superbly outstanding courses in their respective regions.

Foremost among the many events managed by Danner-Eller Golf Properties is the Sara Lee Classic. Founded in 1987 and held annually at the Hermitage, the Sara Lee Classic has grown to be one of the most respected events on the LPGA schedule. Held in late spring, the tournament regularly attracts the leading women players and consistently delivers some of the largest galleries in all of professional golf. Notable winners of the event include Nancy Lopez, Laura Davies, and Michelle McGann, who garnered her first professional win here.

The owners of the Hermitage recently purchased land adjacent to the Hermitage course and have retained the services of heralded architect Denis Griffiths to design a second 18th-hole course. Among Griffith's many outstanding designs in the region is the acclaimed Chateau Elan course in the Atlanta area. The new course is slated to open in the spring of 2000, and the existing clubhouse will be renovated and expanded to accommodate the additional play generated by the new course.

In an area rich in historical sites, the Hermitage is sure to follow in the footsteps and become a must-play course. From bluegrass and grassroots to green grass fairways and sculpted grass greens, the Hermitage has it all.

Furman University
GREENVILLE, SC

Occasionally, it is in the face of the strongest adversities that the most rewarding ideas are fostered. Such was the case for Furman University in Greenville, South Carolina. In the throes of the Great Depression, Furman was forced to implement austere measures in order to survive slowing enrollment and the inability of its students to pay their tuition, both consequences of the failing economy.

Keeping its focus on academics, the administration elected to reduce spending on high priced intercollegiate fall and winter team sports, resulting in the dismissal of the football coaches and discontinuation of athletic scholarships. Furman shifted its emphasis to intramural and less expensive spring sports, like golf, promoting it from club status to a varsity sport in 1932. It is unlikely that anyone at that time could have imagined what would result from a beginning born of such necessity. Golf, chosen primarily because of its affordability, would turn out to be one of the brightest stars in the Furman crown.

In the early 1950s, Furman began building a new campus on 750 acres remotely located at the foot of Paris Mountain. Convinced of the value of athletics in partnership with academics, college president Dr. John Plyler wanted to incorporate sports facilities as an integral part of the new campus. Due in part to Furman's

10th Hole
By Diane Selby

249

consistently high ranking in league and tournament play, the university approved construction of a golf course, and it was decided that the gently sloping hills west of the main campus would be the perfect place for the course. Fittingly, the original concept of the course was determined by the need to keep costs at a minimum.

Dr. Plyler and college vice-president Francis Bonner walked the land and visualized the course. "We actually laid out the first three holes," Bonner says. "Plyler said we should dam up the stream that ran nearby and make it a water hazard, and that's how the pond at the third hole was created." Although never having been involved with golf course design or construction before, university staff members were almost exclusively responsible for the entire project. Campus designers General Robert Dean and R.K. Webel enlisted the aid of Walter Cosby, grounds superintendent for the Greenbriar Hotel in West Virginia, as the only outside consultant. Webel and Cosby staked out the holes and determined the locations of the greens.

Construction began in 1955, manned by the university's resident engineer and a crew of other Furman employees. The first nine holes, completed in 1956, were built without irrigation or drainage, simply by pushing up dirt to create elevated greens that sloped enough to allow for surface drainage. The second nine were added three years later. By today's standards, the methods used by Furman would seem primitive indeed, but in the 1950s, the course set Furman apart as one of only a few universities

that had their own golf courses on campus. In the early 1960s, Furman's golf teams were practicing and playing home matches on their own turf. The men's team placed second in the Southern Conference in 1962, and again in 1969, with a record 19 wins. Furman's men's team finished first four times in 18 years, and have finished in the top five for 29 consecutive years.

The women's golf team was organized in 1972 and proceeded to win every match in their inaugural season, while placing 11th in the National Intercollegiate Women's Golf Championship. Improving to fifth in 1975, they worked even harder and captured the AIAW national championship the following year. They have won the Southern Conference team championship each year since

As its golfers and teams improved, Furman's collegiate golf course was also refined. An irrigation system was added to maintain the bent grass which replaced the original Bermuda; bunkers were redesigned; and the addition of new tees lengthened the course. In 1996, a pro shop was built, and the course opened to the public. The enhancements opened the door for several prestigious golf tournaments, including the Furman Intercollegiate, the Lady Paladin Invitational, the Furman Pro-Am, and the annual State High School Championship.

Furman's commitment to the sport has attracted a host of talented student players who sought the opportunities available at Furman for decades. Members of both the men's and women's teams have gone on to individual success, winning a long list of honors in both amateur and professional tournaments. Some notable Furman graduates include Brad Faxon, Betsy King, Dottie Pepper, and Beth Daniels.

When the first brush strokes of golf were tentatively placed on the Furman canvas, cost effectiveness was the predominant rationale for its choice. During the 70 years since, golf has become one of Furman's dominant colors, a flag that it waves proudly as a symbol of humankind's ancient struggle to overcome adversity and thrive.

Furman Bell Tower
By Diane Selby

8th Hole
By Adriano Manocchia

White Columns

ALPHARETTA, GA

In 1991, Hajime Yamazaki of the Fuji Development Company won an award from "Golf Digest" for Best New Private Course in America. His golf club of Georgia, Lakeside Course, was getting high praise across the country and was compared in some reviews to another layout to the east, Augusta National.

This enthusiastic golfer and developer expanded his vision and set his sights on building the finest public course in Georgia. Based on his earlier success, he was able to attract the best architect available, Tom Fazio.

Mr. Yamazaki gave Fazio a majestic piece of property in the North Atlanta suburb of Alpharetta. The huge canvas included a former equestrian layout, farmland lush with sparkling creeks, and best of all, the opportunity to build something special. The vision would soon become the reality known as White Columns Golf Club.

Yamazaki showed great respect for Fazio's design talents when he allowed him to work his 18-hole design anywhere he wanted. Fazio would later say, "I had 850 acres to work with, and Mr. Yamazaki asked me where the holes would go. What an extraordinary project that starts out that way. I've never been involved in a project where we had so much time, freedom, and land."

In mid-1993, Fazio delivered his routing plan, and the

clearing process began. On a cold and rainy day in December of 1993, Yamazaki's American managers surveyed the muddy outline of the par five, 13th hole. Thick forests lined both sides of the fairway and a beautiful lake was visible in the mist behind the green. Even in the miserable weather, they were struck by just how marvelous the finished product would be, and they were right – it is marvelous. Each hole on the course was sodded, almost unheard of for a public course, but definitely in keeping with Yamazaki's vision of creating the finest public course possible.

Almost a year later, on November 17, 1994, Yamazaki's vision was unveiled. Fazio seemed both overwhelmed at the finished product and proud of the work he had done. His comments reflect his pride in the successful completion of the project. He stated, "From my first day of involvement with the White Columns project I was impressed with the attention to detail. We have so much variety and quality in every hole...that we now have a total golf environment that is not just highlighted by only one signature hole. I certainly look forward to golfers playing the White Columns Golf Club. I know how good it is. Golfers will be pleasantly shocked. White Columns is as good as any golf course, anywhere." High praise indeed from arguably the world's premier golf course architect.

White Columns quickly moved into the upper echelon of top courses in both Georgia and the rest of the United States. The course is rated among the top ten places you can play by "Golf Magazine," and was designated the 6th Best New Public Course in America by "Golf Digest" in 1995, and the eighth Best Course in Georgia in 1997. Locally, "The Atlanta Journal/Constitution" has proclaimed it to be the number one public course in Atlanta.

Neither Fazio nor Yamazaki skimped when it came to the practice facilities. There are six beautifully manicured target greens, practice bunkers, two putting and chipping greens, and a separate instruction area. Said Fazio, "Most people used to feel that practice ranges at private courses were better than at public courses. But that's changed now and the practice range at White Columns is as good as any practice range anywhere. It's so inviting and as high a quality as any hole we designed at White Columns."

First-class amenities complement the award-winning course at White Columns. The clubhouse is large and beautifully appointed, with a well-stocked pro shop, cozy grill room, locker rooms and showers, and an award winning golf pavilion for post round conversation. White Columns boasts all the accouterments befitting a private club, but true to Yamazaki's original vision, Fazio's classic will remain accessible to everyone.

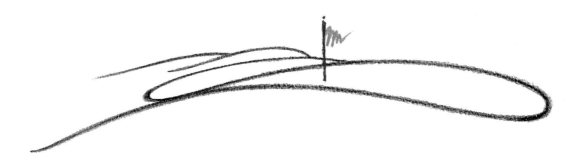

Golf Widow
By Walt Spitzmiller